SYSTEMATIC COUNTRY DIAGNOSTICS

Boosting Shared Prosperity in Chad

Pathways Forward in a Landlocked
Country Beset by Fragility and Conflict

FULBERT TCHANA TCHANA, ABOUDRAHYME SAVADOGO,
AND CLAUDIA NOUMEDEM TEMGOUA

© 2022 International Bank for Reconstruction and Development / The World Bank
1818 H Street NW, Washington, DC 20433
Telephone: 202-473-1000; Internet: www.worldbank.org

Some rights reserved

1 2 3 4   25 24 23 22

Books in this series are published to communicate the results of World Bank research, analysis, and operational experience with the least possible delay. The extent of language editing varies from book to book.

This work is a product of the staff of The World Bank with external contributions. The findings, interpretations, and conclusions expressed in this work do not necessarily reflect the views of The World Bank, its Board of Executive Directors, or the governments they represent. The World Bank does not guarantee the accuracy, completeness, or currency of the data included in this work and does not assume responsibility for any errors, omissions, or discrepancies in the information, or liability with respect to the use of or failure to use the information, methods, processes, or conclusions set forth. The boundaries, colors, denominations, and other information shown on any map in this work do not imply any judgment on the part of The World Bank concerning the legal status of any territory or the endorsement or acceptance of such boundaries.

Nothing herein shall constitute or be construed or considered to be a limitation upon or waiver of the privileges and immunities of The World Bank, all of which are specifically reserved.

Rights and Permissions

This work is available under the Creative Commons Attribution 3.0 IGO license (CC BY 3.0 IGO) http://creativecommons.org/licenses/by/3.0/igo. Under the Creative Commons Attribution license, you are free to copy, distribute, transmit, and adapt this work, including for commercial purposes, under the following conditions:

Attribution—Please cite the work as follows: Tchana Tchana, Fulbert, Aboudrahyme Savadogo, and Claudia Noumedem Temgoua. 2022. *Boosting Shared Prosperity in Chad: Pathways Forward in a Landlocked Country Beset by Fragility and Conflict.* Systematic Country Diagnostics. Washington, DC: World Bank. doi:10.1596/978-1-4648-1886-8. License: Creative Commons Attribution CC BY 3.0 IGO

Translations—If you create a translation of this work, please add the following disclaimer along with the attribution: *This translation was not created by The World Bank and should not be considered an official World Bank translation. The World Bank shall not be liable for any content or error in this translation.*

Adaptations—If you create an adaptation of this work, please add the following disclaimer along with the attribution: *This is an adaptation of an original work by The World Bank. Views and opinions expressed in the adaptation are the sole responsibility of the author or authors of the adaptation and are not endorsed by The World Bank.*

Third-party content—The World Bank does not necessarily own each component of the content contained within the work. The World Bank therefore does not warrant that the use of any third-party-owned individual component or part contained in the work will not infringe on the rights of those third parties. The risk of claims resulting from such infringement rests solely with you. If you wish to re-use a component of the work, it is your responsibility to determine whether permission is needed for that re-use and to obtain permission from the copyright owner. Examples of components can include, but are not limited to, tables, figures, or images.

All queries on rights and licenses should be addressed to World Bank Publications, The World Bank Group, 1818 H Street NW, Washington, DC 20433, USA; e-mail: pubrights@worldbank.org.

ISBN: 978-1-4648-1886-8
DOI: 10.1596/978-1-4648-1886-8

Cover photo: Rocher de l'éléphant – Tchad, © Fulbert Tchana Tchana / World Bank. Used with permission; further permission required for reuse.
Cover design: Debra Naylor / Naylor Design Inc.

Contents

Foreword   vii
Acknowledgments   ix
Executive Summary   xi
Abbreviations   xix

Introduction   1
   Note   2

CHAPTER 1   Progress toward the Twin Goals since 2015   3
   Overview   3
   Country and economic context   3
   Poverty trends   8
   Nonmonetary poverty   14
   Inequality and shared prosperity   22
   Low access to employment   23
   Notes   25
   References   25

CHAPTER 2   Binding Constraints on Poverty Reduction and Shared Prosperity   27
   Overview   27
   Constraints identified in 2015 that remain   27
   Growing constraints not covered by the 2015 SCD   36
   Notes   41
   References   41

CHAPTER 3   Key Prerequisites to Seize Opportunities   43
   Overview   43
   Addressing constraints   43
   Strengthening the social contract through accountable and inclusive institutions   44
   Adapting to climate change and improving the management of natural resources   47
   Achieving adequate macrofiscal management and a business-friendly environment   50
   Notes   53
   References   53

CHAPTER 4 **Key Pathways** 55
  Overview 55
  Strengthen human capital and reduce the gender gap 55
  Improve infrastructure for better service delivery 61
  Promote diversification and sectors with jobs potential 65
  Notes 69
  References 69

CHAPTER 5 **Knowledge Gaps** 71
  Note 74

Appendix A **Benchmarks for Chad Systematic Country Diagnostic** 75

Appendix B **Stakeholders for Chad Consultations** 77

Figures

ES.1 Summary of the systematic country diagnostic narrative   xv
1.1   Population trends, by age group, 1980–2050   4
1.2   Population, by age and gender, 2019   5
1.3   Refugees and internally displaced persons in Chad, 2014–20   6
1.4   GDP per capita trends, 2014–20   7
1.5   GDP per capita, PPP, 2000–20   7
1.6   GDP growth, 2010–20   8
1.7   Trends in national poverty measures, 2003, 2011, and 2018   9
1.8   Poverty incidence and number of poor people, by location, 2011 and 2018   10
1.9   Trends in poverty rates, by agroecological zone, 2011 and 2018   10
1.10 Trends in poverty rates, by region, 2011 and 2018   11
1.11 Gross primary enrollment, 2003, 2015, and 2018   14
1.12 Net secondary enrollment, 2018   15
1.13 Gross tertiary enrollment, 2017   16
1.14 Reasons for not attending school, children ages 6–17, 2018   16
1.15 Reasons for not attending school, girls ages 14–19, 2018   17
1.16 Maternal health and fertility rates   19
1.17 Ownership of assets, 2011 and 2018   20
1.18 Access to basic services, by location, 2011 and 2018   20
1.19 Access to basic services, Chad and comparator countries, 2017–18   21
1.20 Mortality rate attributed to unsafe water, unsafe sanitation, and lack of hygiene, 2016   21
1.21 Growth incidence curves, 2011–18   22
1.22 Occupational category of employed population, ages 15+, 2018   24
1.23 Proportion of first-time job seekers among unemployed, ages 15+, 2018   24
2.1   Access to basic services, Chad and comparator countries, 2017–18   28
2.2   Access to basic services, by location, 2011 and 2018   29
2.3   Main challenges facing the electricity sector in Chad   29
2.4   Poverty head count, by number of children per household, 2018   33
2.5   Poverty head count, by gender of household head, 2018   33
2.6   Government revenue, 2010–20   38
2.7   Fiscal and current account balances, 2010–20   39

Maps

1.1   Geographic distribution of monetary poverty head count ratio, 2018   12
1.2   Geographic distribution of multidimensional poverty index, 2018   13
2.1   Political violence in Chad, by event type, 2013–20   37

Tables

2.1	Key service delivery indicators	35
2.2	Transparency Indexes, Chad and selected groups	36
4.1	The World Bank Group's energy program in Chad	63
5.1	Advisory services and analytics in Chad, 2016–21	72
A.1	Systematic Country Diagnostic benchmark list, Chad	75
B.1	Stakeholder consultations in Chad, September 13–17, 2021	77

Foreword

I am pleased to present the book version of Chad's 2022 Systematic Country Diagnostic (SCD) update, *Boosting Shared Prosperity in Chad: Pathways Forward in a Landlocked Country Beset by Fragility and Conflict*. With this version, the World Bank intends to bring economic knowledge on Chad closer to a broader audience, including the research community interested in the country economic issues.

This book provides new information on progress toward reducing poverty and boosting shared prosperity in Chad by revisiting the overall framework and pathways laid out in the 2015 SCD. It leverages recent works to provide a more granular set of policy priorities to address the identified constraints to achieving the World Bank's twin goals in the country. This 2022 SCD update is a critical input to the upcoming Country Engagement Note (CEN).

This book identifies eight constraints that thwart economic growth and poverty reduction. These include five binding constraints already identified in 2015: (a) weak human capital and slow demographic transition, (b) weak productivity and social return on rural economic activities, (c) low access to infrastructure and services, (d) higher gender inequality, and (e) poor quality of public administration services. Three new constraints emerged during the last five years: (a) violence and fragility; (b) oil revenue volatility, weak macroeconomic management, and debt sustainability issues; and (c) environment and climate change.

This book proposes substantial reforms to overcome the constraints and accelerate poverty reduction. The three pathways identified address (a) increasing human capital accumulation, with a focus on gender inclusion; (b) improving infrastructure for better service delivery; and (c) promoting economic diversification and sectors with a strategic advantage to create more and better jobs. However, the success of the reforms will depend on the country's capacity (a) to strengthen social contract through accountable and inclusive institutions, (b) to address climate change and improve the management of natural resources, and (c) to achieve adequate macrofiscal management and a business-friendly environment.

This book is being published at a critical moment in the country's history. Chad is in a political transition and a national dialogue process involving almost every layer of the society. If successful, this process would promote peace and stability, which are essential for economic development. I hope this book will also contribute to these efforts as the World Bank continues to support the country under the IDA20.

Raşit Pertev
Country Manager, Chad
The World Bank

Acknowledgments

The compilation of this Systematic Country Diagnostic (SCD) was led by Fulbert Tchana Tchana (senior economist), Aboudrahyme Savadogo (economist), and Claudia Noumedem Temgoua (economist), with a core team comprising Jean Pierre Chauffour (program leader), Pierre Xavier Bonneau (lead transport specialist and program leader), Christophe Rockmore (practice leader), Micky O. Ananth (operations analyst), Theresa Bampoe (program assistant), and Nicola Amadai (program assistant).

The core team relied on sector-specific expertise from colleagues across the World Bank Group's Global Practices (GPs) and Cross-Cutting Solutions Areas (CCSAs). The table below identifies the team members who represent each of these GPs and CCSAs, whose specific knowledge of and experience in the context of Chad provided expert input throughout the SCD process.

GLOBAL PRACTICE OR GLOBAL THEME	TEAM MEMBER(S)
Agriculture	Ziva Razafintsalama
Education	Harisoa Danielle Rasolonjatovo Andriamihamina, Zacharie Ngueng
Energy	Yuriy Myroshnychenko, Abdou Toure, Alexis L. E. Madelain
Environment and Forestry	Aurelie Marie Simone Monique Rossignol, Ellysar Baroudy
Extractives	Silvana Tordo
Finance, Competitiveness, and Innovation	Mamoudou Nagnalen Barry
Fragility, Conflict, and Violence	Rebecca Lacroix, Catalina Quintero
Gender	Daniel John Kirkwood
Governance	Kandi Magendo, Ousmane Maurice Megnan Kolie, Monique Ndome Didiba, Sidy Diop
Health, Nutrition, and Population	Andy Tembo, Jean-Claude Taptue, Nicola Rosemberg
International Finance Corporation	Sabri Youcef Draia, Volker Treichel, Julie Lohi, Cesar Baira Dering, Inoussa De Youba Ouedraogo, Konan Jean Marcel Niankoun
Legal	Sophie Wernert
Macroeconomics, Trade, and Investment	Fulbert Tchana Tchana, Claudia Noumedem Temgoua, Koami D. Amegble, Olanrewaju Kassim
Poverty and Equity	Aboudrahyme Savadogo, Clarence Tsimpo, Nadia Belhaj Hassine Belghith

GLOBAL PRACTICE OR GLOBAL THEME	TEAM MEMBER(S)
Private Sector Development, Trade, Competitiveness, and Economic Diversification	Cesar Baira Dering, Kathryn Hulseman, Francine Fernandez
Social Sector Development	Claudia Zambra Taibo
Telecommunication	Tounwende Alain Sawadogo
Transport	Danye Aboki
Urban, Resilience, and Land	Nathalie Andrea Wandel, Oscar A. Ishizawa, Cecile Lorillou
Water	Aude-Sophie Rodella, Taibou Maiga, François Bertone

The team is grateful to the peer reviewers—Mark Andrew Dutz (lead economist), Allen Dennis (program leader), Yutaka Yoshino (lead country economist), Nandini Krishnan (senior economist), Aly Sanoh (senior economist), Pablo Fajnzylber (director, Strategy and Operations, Infrastructure), Franck Bousquet (senior director, Fragility, Conflict, and Violence), Soukeyna Kane (director, Fragility, Conflict, and Violence), Reynaldo F. Pastor (chief counsel), Alberto Rodriguez (director, Strategy and Operations, Human Development), Hoveida Nobakht (acting senior director, Sustainable Development), Simeon K. Ehui (regional director, Sustainable Development), and Hana Brixi (global director, Gender)—as well as to the Climate Change Group for their insightful constructive comments. The team is also grateful to Oscar Parlback for his editorial support and to Rolf Parta for his internal and external stakeholder consultation facilitation.

Finally, we would like to thank Clara Ana Coutinho de Sousa (country director), Abebe Adugna Dadi (regional director), Rasit Pertev (country manager), Kofi Nouve (operations manager), Theo David Thomas (practice manager), Johan A. Mistiaen (practice manager), Yue Man Lee (lead economist), and Faruk Khan (economic adviser) for their guidance, support, and comments.

Throughout the SCD process, the team consulted with and received input from Aboubakar Adam Ibrahim (Directeur Général de l'Economie, Ministère de l'Economie, de la Planification du Développement, et de la Coopération Internationale—MPEDCI), Douzounet Mallaye (Directeur des Analyses et des Etudes Prospectives, MPEDCI), Gadom Djal Gadom (Directeur des Stratégies et Politiques Economiques, MPEDCI), Dobingar Allesembaye (Directeur General des Etudes et Prévisions, MPEDCI), and Saleh Idriss Goukouni (Directeur des Etudes et la Prévisions, Ministère des Finances et du Budget). The team also benefited from the input of the participants at the semivirtual stakeholders' consultations held September 13–17, 2021, in N'Djamena (a full list of participants is included in appendix B).

Executive Summary

Chad's economy has contracted since 2015, preventing the country from reducing poverty and improving development outcomes.

Chad remains among the least developed countries in the world, and its GDP per capita has contracted since 2015. Its gross domestic product (GDP) per capita (in constant 2010 US dollars) was US$710 in 2019, down significantly from US$961 in 2014 and lower than the average of US$840 and US$1,590 in low-income countries and Sub-Saharan Africa (SSA), respectively. Mirroring this poor economic performance, the country ranked 187th out of 189 countries on the Human Development Index in 2020, and access to basic services and infrastructure is low compared to regional and structural peers.

Progress on reducing poverty has stalled since 2015, and the number of extreme poor has increased, with both trends exacerbated by the COVID-19 (coronavirus) pandemic. Although the extreme poverty rate declined between 2011 and 2018, progress stalled since 2015 and the COVID-19 pandemic reversed some of the gains in 2020. Furthermore, the number of extreme poor increased from 5.8 million in 2011 to 6.5 million in 2018 because of rapid population growth and modest progress in reducing the poverty rate. Simulations also suggest that the pandemic pushed an additional 0.8 million people into poverty in 2020. Poverty is concentrated in rural areas, and extreme poverty is high among households working in agriculture and those living in or near areas affected by conflict.

Multidimensional poverty remains prevalent. The incidence of multidimensional poverty has declined modestly during the last decade, but the level of deprivation among households remains severe along several dimensions, including primary school enrollment (75.7 percent), illiteracy (88.7 percent), and access to basic services (90 percent). Almost the entire rural population lacks access to the electrical grid, while 40 percent of all households and 46 percent of rural households only have access to unsafe drinking water sources. Due to the severe gaps in access to basic services, the number of deaths attributed to unsafe water and sanitation and lack of hygiene was the highest among comparator countries in 2016 (with the mortality rate attributed to these sources in Chad 1.4 times higher than in Mali). The country also continues to experience a high fertility rate (5.7 births per woman in 2018, among the highest globally and higher than the Sub-Saharan Africa average of 4.8), with serious consequences for women's health.

Low access to formal employment, exacerbated by population growth in urban and semiurban centers, has characterized the lack of development progress. Despite relatively high rates of employment (73 percent of the total population aged 15 years and above are active in the labor force), over 90 percent of the employed population is either self-employed or employed by households, only an estimated 3 percent works in managerial positions or as employers, and 1.7 percent works as skilled labor. The rise of the urban and semi-urban population and educated youth has not been matched by a proportional increase in formal employment. Most workers are employed in low-skill occupations, while youth comprise most of the country's unemployed and discouraged workers. Self-employment and occupations with relatively low productivity dominate employment, and employment rates vary widely between N'Djamena and other urban and rural areas.

The analysis in this SCD Update confirms that the five binding constraints identified in the 2015 SCD continue to thwart economic growth and poverty reduction in Chad:

1. **Human capital remains weak, and the demographic transition has been slow.** Chad's Human Capital Index[1] (HCI)—a measure of the amount of human capital that children born today can expect to attain by age 18, given the risks of poor health and poor education that prevail in their countries—was only 0.3 in 2020, almost the same as in 2010. This means that children born in Chad in 2020 could expect to attain only 30 percent of their potential as adults, which places Chad near the bottom of the global HCI distribution. The country's primary school completion rate is well below the SSA average, and its child, infant, and maternal mortality ratios are among the world's highest. Chad's weak performance on the HCI is partly explained by underinvestment in health and education and its slow demographic transition (due to the high fertility rate), which puts additional pressure on the limited resources available.

2. **Productivity and the incomes from economic activity in rural areas continue to be low.** Agriculture and livestock are the main economic activities in rural areas, and households relying on these activities for their livelihoods are more likely to be poor. Lack of public investment, adequate tools and technology, and improved water and land management has led to relatively small landholdings and low productivity gains in agriculture. Meanwhile, poorly organized value chains and weak export capacity also undermine productivity in agriculture and livestock activities.

3. **Low and volatile infrastructure investments have resulted in low access to basic services.** Chad has one of the lowest rates of electricity access in the world. In 2018, only an estimated 8 percent of the population had access to electricity, much lower than the SSA average of 48 percent, with significant disparities between urban (20 percent) and rural (4 percent) areas. In 2015, only 10 percent of the population benefited from adequate sanitation services, compared to the SSA average of 28 percent, while only 6 percent of Chadians had access to the internet, compared to the averages of 22 percent

and 15 percent for SSA and low-income countries, respectively. Public investment has also been volatile and procyclical, usually tied to oil prices, thereby undermining its efficiency and effectiveness. Cuts in investment expenditures have been particularly costly for Chad, given its low capital stock and subsequent low social sector performance.

4. **Gender inequality in Chad is among the highest in the world, and little progress has been made since 2015.** Women and girls face inequality in all aspects of life. Significant gaps exist between boys and girls in secondary education, and more than two out of three girls are married as children to adult men. The interconnection between school dropouts, early marriage, gender-based violence, and early childbearing becomes more prominent as girls reach adolescence, negatively affecting women's human capital and productivity. While the maternal mortality rate dropped from 1,450 deaths per 100,000 live births in 1990 to 1,140 in 2017, it remains high and far from the Sustainable Development Goal of 70 by 2030. Moreover, women's ability to contribute to and benefit from economic opportunities is undermined by large gender gaps in agricultural productivity, enterprise performance, and employment.

5. **The quality of public administration services is weak and has deteriorated since 2015.** In terms of service delivery, Chad performs worse than the average of regional comparators. Service delivery is limited, costly, and constrained by the large size of the country, the sparse population density, and slow and disorderly urbanization. Moreover, government effectiveness is constrained by limited public administration capacity, a concentration of resources and decision-making in the capital city, low levels of revenues, and sensitivity to shocks such as COVID-19. The reduction of public employee benefits due to the recent economic crisis has led to numerous strikes, reducing the quality of public services.

This SCD update identifies three additional binding constraints that increasingly undermine progress toward poverty reduction:

1. **Insecurity and conflict have risen sharply since 2015 due to the proliferation of both internal and external sources of insecurity.** Chad finds itself amid an ongoing political transition due to the passing of President Déby on April 20, 2021. External sources of risk include (a) spillovers from regional conflicts and forced displacement (including from conflicts in the Lake Chad region, Libya, the Central African Republic, and Sudan); (b) geopolitical influence from foreign sovereign and private interventions; and (c) the activities of transnational criminal groups. Internal drivers of fragility include (a) hypercentralized and noninclusive governance; (b) regional imbalances and exclusion that fuel grievances; (c) elite capture, poor governance, and low capacity for local participation in the oil sector, which fuel inequality and exclusion; (d) security sector dysfunction and weak rule of law that prevent the effective implementation of justice and mitigation of conflicts; and (e) intercommunal tensions that are exacerbated by increasing natural resource scarcity and climate change. While Chad has historically been affected by instability, the extent and multifaceted nature of its insecurity and conflict result in a renewed sense of urgency to address the drivers of fragility, conflict, and violence (FCV) (World Bank 2019).

2. **Chad's economic development suffers from oil revenue volatility, inadequate macroeconomic management of economic shocks, and unsustainable debt.** Oil revenue volatility has been a major determinant of the country's negative growth dynamic in recent years, and it has led to the adoption of painful fiscal consolidation programs (World Bank 2018). The absence of a clear strategy for managing oil price volatility hampers Chad's capacity to take full advantage of its oil resources. Moreover, the COVID-19 crisis and its related shocks have emphasized the dangers of an overreliance on oil revenue to ensure fiscal sustainability and economic growth. Despite debt restructuring in 2015 and 2018, Chad has been facing a high risk of debt distress since 2017. The most recent World Bank–International Monetary Fund Debt Sustainability Analysis in 2020 pointed to an unsustainable debt situation, and another episode of debt restructuring started in 2021.
3. **Vulnerability to climate change in Chad is among the highest in the world.**[2] Climate change contributes to desertification; the degradation of forests, soil, and natural habitats; the loss of biodiversity; the depletion of water tables; and the silting of oases. Climate change also exacerbates more frequent episodes of drought and flooding. This growing climate vulnerability further heightens insecurity.[3]

The SCD proposes six solution areas to address the binding constraints on poverty reduction (see figure ES.1). The first set includes three cross-cutting prerequisites that are critical to strengthen the social contract, improve the management of natural resources, and adapt to climate change; and achieve adequate macrofiscal management as well as a business-friendly environment. These prerequisites are particularly important to address constraints associated with conflict, oil price's volatility, climate change, and weak public administration. The second set of solutions includes three pathways aimed at raising worker productivity and improving access to improved earning opportunities: (a) supporting improvements in human capital to improve worker productivity, (b) improving Infrastructure to raise productivity, and (c) promoting sectors with a strategic advantage for more and better jobs.

The success of reform efforts will depend on the ability to address FCV drivers, adapt to climate change, promote an adequate macrofiscal framework, and create a business-friendly regulatory environment

Prerequisite 1: Strengthening the social contract through accountable and inclusive institutions[4]

To change the medium-term trajectory of growth and poverty reduction and address the country's fragility challenges, the authorities need to strengthen governance, notably the trust between citizens and the government. Although violence in Chad has a strong cross-border and regional component, current conflict risks also originate in deep-rooted structural causes. To reduce the likelihood of conflict, the government needs to strengthen inclusive and transparent governance at the national and subnational levels and reinforce the rule of law, justice, and dispute resolution mechanisms. Moreover, to address the country's fragility challenges, public policies should aim to build capacity to deliver basic services; expand government technology solutions; provide core services in low-density and insecure areas; ensure government continuity during crises

FIGURE ES.1
Summary of the systematic country diagnostic narrative

Objective: Boost inclusive economic growth and poverty reduction

Progress toward the twin goals since 2015
- Poverty reduction stalled due to multiple economic crises
- GDP per-capita contracted
- Limited job creation, particularly in formal sectors

Previously identified constraints
- Weak human capital and slow demographic transition
- Weak productivity and social return on rural economic activities
- Low access to infrastructure and services
- Higher gender inequality
- Weak quality of public administration services

Growing constraints
- Violence and fragility
- Oil revenue volatility, weak macroeconomic management, and debt sustainability issues
- Environment and climate change

Prerequisites

Prerequisite 1: Strengthening social contract through accountable and inclusive institutions
Prerequisite 2: Addressing climate change and improving the management of natural resources
Prerequisite 3: Achieving adequate macrofiscal management and a business-friendly environment

Pathways

Strengthen human capital and reduce gender gap
- Improving access to and quality of education and training
- Improving the performance of the health care and education systems
- Empowering women and accelerating the demographic transition
- Enhancing social protection programs

Improve infrastructure and service delivery
- Reforming the energy sector for greater access
- Improving the efficiency of the water sector
- Improving transport infrastructure and logistics services
- Expanding the telecommunications network

Promote diversification and sectors with jobs potential
- Promoting agriculture, livestock, food, and meat-processing industries
- Promoting the digital economy, increasing access to credit, and promoting digital payments

Poverty reduction and shared prosperity

Source: World Bank.

such as the COVID-19 pandemic; and curb corruption by improving the accountability of public services.

Prerequisite 2: Adapting to climate change and improving the management of natural resources
Both the impact of climate change and measures to adapt and, to the extent possible, mitigate it are cross-sectoral. The country's natural capital assets need to be well maintained to strengthen the functioning of ecosystems and the productivity of economic activities (for example, agriculture and livestock), as well as to improve Chad's economic resilience to climate change. For example, increasing the tree cover around agricultural areas retains soil, dampens flooding effects, increases the fertility of soil, and provides shade. Climate change is contributing to higher temperatures and more frequent flood and drought

cycles, which are likely to affect the poor the most.[5] This implies that government should ensure that future investments in infrastructure such as energy, roads, telecommunications, and water distribution increase the country's resilience to climate change. In addition, fiscal and monetary policies that avoid exchange rate overvaluation and favor credit to the private sector and improving the transparency and efficiency of oil revenue and exploitation (for example, by adopting fiscal rules) will help Chad benefit better from its natural resources.

Prerequisite 3: Achieving adequate macrofiscal management and a business-friendly environment

To ensure the adequacy of Chad's macroeconomic framework and accelerate economic growth, the country needs to pursue debt restructuring, reform the public investment system, and strengthen regional integration. Debt restructuring efforts need to include a reduction of the country's net present value and could benefit from the adoption of the G20 common framework. Domestic fiscal policies should focus on mobilizing non-oil revenues (for example, by improving the value-added tax), and improve the efficiency of public procurement functions (for example, by improving the planning, budgeting, and implementation of public investments). Moreover, Chad needs to strengthen economic integration with coastal and neighboring countries to improve its competitiveness. For example, it should adopt validated business-friendly reforms, increase the availability of economic data, and improve coordination on development projects and service delivery.

Pathways to accelerate poverty reduction focus on human capital, infrastructure, and sectors with strategic advantages

Pathway 1: Strengthen human capital and reduce the gender gap[6]

Reforms are needed to strengthen human capital and reduce the gender gap. This will require increasing access to quality education and health care and improving the targeting of the social protection system. This can be done by (a) recruiting and deploying qualified teachers and health professionals across all regions; (b) providing relevant education and health inputs, equipment, and infrastructure; (c) increasing the efficiency of the training system to serve the country's labor market needs; (d) prioritizing maternal, reproductive, neonatal, child, and adolescent health care; (e) adopting policies to support women's entrepreneurship and empowerment; and (f) increasing investment in social protection and service delivery systems to expand coverage and enhance the coordination of safety net programs which can serve as platforms for other demand-side interventions and for climate resilience.

Pathway 2: Improve infrastructure for better service delivery

Chad needs to build and maintain key infrastructure in energy, water, transport, and telecommunications to improve access to basic services and markets. This will require efforts to (a) improve the technical and financial oversight of the country's state-owned enterprises for more effective and efficient service delivery; (b) increase private sector participation in infrastructure sectors; (c) reduce regional inequality through improved spatial planning; and (d) make infrastructure more resilient to disasters, given Chad's vulnerability to climate change. While the country needs to improve road maintenance and the governance of public water utility companies, improving access to energy is the country's highest priority. Potential energy reforms include developing the regional power trade market, increasing local generation capacity; transitioning from high-cost diesel to heavy fuel oil or renewable sources for electricity production; increasing access to modern electricity services (grid and off-grid); and reforming the public utility company, Société Nationale d'Electricité (SNE).

Pathway 3: Promote diversification and sectors with jobs potential

Chad's reforms need to promote sectors with strategic advantages and high job-creation potential. According to the parallel and complementary Country Private Sector Diagnostic (CPSD) (IFC 2021), Chad has a revealed comparative advantage in selected agricultural products (for example, livestock, gum arabic, sesame seed, and cotton), oil, and extractives. Based on an evaluation of employment elasticity, prospects for domestic value addition, and economic diversification, Chad could expect high economic and social returns from investing in six strategic sectors: agriculture, livestock, oil sector lateral links, green economy, agroprocessing, and digital economy and financial inclusion. To achieve the full potential of these sectors, technological innovation and regulatory reforms will be needed. To address the above-mentioned low productivity and income from agriculture, national land reform will be needed to increase agricultural productivity and adopting. The country should also fully implement the Economic and Monetary Community of Central Africa (Communauté Économique et Monétaire de l'Afrique Centrale, CEMAC) livestock regulations which, in conjunction with the organization of stakeholders along the value chain, will be instrumental to the livestock sector. The government should also reform its fiscal policy to promote the proliferation of digital payment options, which could improve access to credit and financial inclusion.

NOTES

1. The index value varies between 0.0 and 1.0.
2. According to the Notre Dame Global Adaptation Initiative (ND-GAIN) Country Index 2021.
3. Chad published its Nationally Determined Contribution (NDC) in October 2021, which embodies is efforts to reduce national emissions and adapt to the impacts of climate change. The NDC aligns also with Chad's Vision 2030.
4. This prerequisite aligns with "Rebuild trust between citizens and the state," one of the four high-level goals of the World Bank's Africa West and Central Region (AFW) Strategy.
5. According to the World Bank's updated Climate Change Action Plan (CCAP), there will be a greater alignment of World Bank financing with a country's nationally determined contributions (NDCs) and the goals of the Paris Agreement. To this end, the World Bank's financing portfolio for Chad will need to further integrate climate resilience, going beyond the initial screening for cobenefits. This in turn will contribute to Chad's implementation of its NDC.
6. This pathway coincides with "Strengthen human capital and empower women," one of the four high-level goals of the World Bank's Africa West and Central Region (AFW) Strategy.

REFERENCES

IFC (International Finance Corporation). 2021. "A Country Private Sector Diagnostic for Chad." World Bank Group, Washington, DC.

World Bank. 2018. "Escaping Chad's Growth Labyrinth: Disentangling Constraints from Opportunities and Finding a Path to Sustainable Growth." World Bank, Washington, DC. https://elibrary.worldbank.org/doi/pdf/10.1596/30941.

World Bank. 2019. "Evaluation des Risques et de la Résilience dans la région du Sahel." Unpublished paper, World Bank, Washington, DC.

Abbreviations

CEMAC	Economic and Monetary Community of Central Africa, Communauté Économique et Monétaire de l'Afrique Centrale
CFAF	Central African CFA franc
COVID-19	coronavirus 2019
FCV	fragility, conflict, and violence
G5 Sahel	Burkina Faso, Chad, Mali, Mauritania, and Niger
GDP	gross domestic product
NDC	Nationally Determined Contribution (under the United Nations Framework Convention on Climate Change)
PFM	public financial management
RCA	revealed comparative advantage
RRA	Risk and Resilience Assessment
SCD	Systematic Country Diagnostic
SDG	Sustainable Development Goal
SOE	state-owned enterprise
SSA	Sub-Saharan Africa
VAT	value-added tax

Introduction

Since Chad's first Systematic Country Diagnostic (SCD) in 2015, the economy has experienced two episodes of economic crisis, including the COVID-19 pandemic that constrained poverty reduction efforts. Between 2015 and 2020, economic growth contracted by an average of 0.3 percent per year, mainly due to low oil revenue and growing regional insecurity. While poverty declined in 2015–18 due to a growing agriculture sector, simulations suggest that the pandemic caused a 5.5 percentage increase in poverty in 2020. In addition, in April 2021, the country began a political transition following the unexpected passing of President Idriss Deby Itno.

The ongoing outbreak of COVID-19 (coronavirus) has exacerbated Chad's economic and societal challenges to unprecedented levels. Compared to countries in Europe, North America, Latin America and the Caribbean, and Southern Africa, the spread of COVID-19 has been relatively limited in Chad so far, with 5,703 cases and 181 deaths, as of November 30, 2021. However, the health, societal, and economic impact of the pandemic will be felt in the coming years, particularly through channels of learning for children and nutrition for the entire population from loss of revenues.

Substantive analytical work conducted since the 2015 SCD has deepened the diagnostic and sharpened the policy priorities. The analytical work included a growth analytics, a Poverty Assessment, a Public Expenditure Review (PER), a gender economics report, a petroleum sector diagnostic, a water sector report, and a Country Private Sector Diagnostic (CPSD).[1] This body of work deepens the previous diagnostic but does not fundamentally modify the general findings of the 2015 SCD. As such, this is an SCD Update to the 2015 SCD.

This SCD Update aims to (a) provide an updated narrative on progress toward the World Bank Group's twin goals of reducing poverty and boosting shared prosperity in Chad, (b) revisit the overall framework and pathways laid out in the previous SCD and make modifications as necessary in light of new information generated by recent analytical work, and (c) leverage recent work to provide a more granular set of policy priorities to address the identified constraints.

The SCD Update uses a four-phase prioritization process of constraints and pathways. First, a rigorous review and analysis of constraints in terms of the World Bank's twin goals was conducted done and summarized in the diagnostic section. Second, the core country team conducted meetings with World Bank task team leaders and counterparts to refine the list of identified binding constraints. Third, the entire country team met at an SCD workshop to discuss and solidify the findings. Fourth, a formal consultation with stakeholders to incorporate feedback and finalize the core binding constraints, pathways, and prerequisites concluded the process.

Finally, this SCD Update will serve as an essential input to the upcoming 2022–26 Country Partnership Framework (CPF). Chad's current CPF was adopted in December 2015 and was scheduled to end in 2020 but was extended to 2022. The 2015 CPF focused on three core areas: (a) strengthening the management of public resources, (b) improving returns to agriculture and building value chains, and (c) developing human capital and reducing vulnerability.

NOTE

1. Chapter 5 includes a complete list of the analytical work.

1 Progress toward the Twin Goals since 2015

OVERVIEW

While the poverty rate fell from 47 percent to 42 percent between 2011 and 2018, the COVID-19 (coronavirus) pandemic has offset the country's progress toward achieving the World Bank's twin's goals of ending extreme poverty and boosting shared prosperity. The incidence of extreme poverty increased by an estimated 5.5 percent in 2020, and multidimensional poverty remains high. Moreover, challenges in access to basic infrastructure and services persist. Access to public services has not improved in recent years, and Chad continues to lag benchmark countries, with gaps especially wide among poor households. In 2018, less than 2 percent of poor households had access to electricity, and 48 percent of poor households lacked access to improved water. Due to the wide gaps in access to basic services, Chad recorded the highest number of deaths among benchmark countries attributable to unsafe water, unsafe sanitation, and lack of hygiene. Indicators for access to education and health care similarly lag, indicating a lack of investment in human capital, and the pandemic and the related economic crisis have further deteriorated these indicators. Furthermore, external and internal drivers of conflict and fragility, as well as climate impacts, have worsened since 2015.

COUNTRY AND ECONOMIC CONTEXT

Chad is a large landlocked country in Central Africa prone to severe weather- and climate-related events. The country has three distinct agroecological zones: the Sahara Desert in the north, the Sahel in the center, and the Sudanese belt in the south. The first covers almost half of the land area but is home to less than 5 percent of the population. As the region is extremely arid, pastoralism is the main livelihood activity. The Sahel region makes up about one-quarter of the land area and contains approximately one-third of the population. This region is also arid but is more suited to agriculture, particularly cereal production. Lake Chad in the Sahelian zone continues to serve as an important source of livelihood and fresh water, although conflict has risen sharply in the basin area, affecting social and economic opportunities. The lake has shrunk considerably since the 1970s, and though it is partly replenishing (Magrin 2016), resources are increasingly scarce, which has an impact on livelihoods. The Sudanese belt in the south, which is more fertile, hosts the majority of Chad's population and almost all of the country's cotton production. With 76 percent of the population living in rural areas, many households depend heavily on agricultural and pastoral activities, driven by heavy rainfall and the availability of groundwater in agroecological zones.

Chad's population is growing quickly, putting pressure on the country's resources. The population is projected to grow from 16 million in 2020 to 22 million and 34 million by 2030 and 2050, respectively (figure 1.1). While the fertility rate fell from 7.4 births per woman in 2000 to an estimated 5.7 births in 2018, it remains significantly higher than the Sub-Saharan African (SSA) average of 4.8 births per woman. As a result, Chad has the third-youngest population in the world: the median age is 16.6 years, with two-thirds of the population estimated to be younger than 25 years old (figure 1.2). Furthermore, the weak capacity of the private sector, coupled with the limited room for increasing payroll budgets, makes it challenging to absorb the large cohort of generally unskilled young job seekers.

Security risks originating in neighboring countries have persistently destabilized the economy. A rebellion caused the death of President Idriss Déby Itno on April 20, 2021, and led to an unanticipated political transition. A transitionary military council (conseil militaire de transition, CMT) was established by military authorities and presided over by General Mahamat Idriss Déby. The president of the CMT also fulfills the role of president of the Republic of Chad. Members of the political opposition, rebel leaders, and civil society have expressed concern over this transition, as it did not follow the constitutional order. The CMT has outlined an 18-month transition period, renewable once, that foresees an inclusive national dialogue and a process to revise the constitution and hold presidential elections. According to the 2021 Chad Risk and Resilience Assessment (RRA), Chad's cross-border fragility risks include (a) regional conflict spillovers and forced displacement, (b) geopolitical influence, and (c) the activities of transnational criminal groups. Continued insecurity in

FIGURE 1.1

Population trends, by age group, 1980–2050

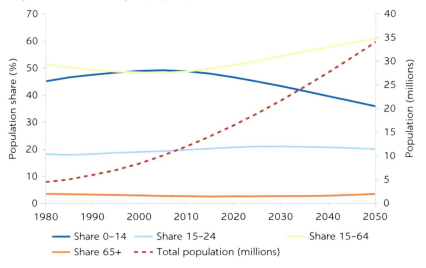

Source: UN DESA 2019.

FIGURE 1.2
Population, by age and gender, 2019

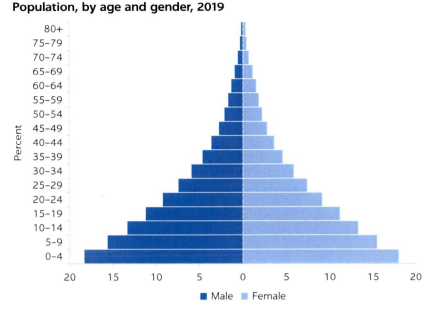

Source: World Development Indicators, https://data.worldbank.org/indicator.

the northeast of Nigeria and new rebel activity in the Tibesti region and along the northern border with Libya forced the government to reinforce security measures while maintaining the country's strong contributions to the Multinational Joint Task Force and the G5 Cross-Border Joint Force.

Moreover, cross-border insecurity has exacerbated more structural fragility drivers, leading to a sharp increase in the number of conflicts since 2015 that have disrupted progress toward the World Bank's twin goals. According to the 2021 Chad RRA, these structural drivers of conflict include (a) hypercentralized and noninclusive governance; (b) regional imbalances and exclusion that fuel grievances; (c) elite capture, poor governance, and low capacity for local participation in the oil sector that fuel inequality and exclusion; (d) security sector dysfunction and weak rule of law that prevent effective implementation of justice and mitigation of conflicts; and (e) intercommunal tensions that are exacerbated by increasing natural resource scarcity and climate change. The government has developed various strategies to address some of these conflict and fragility drivers, including a three-year action plan under the World Bank Group's Prevention and Resilience Allocation.

Insecurity and violence have created an acute humanitarian situation and resulted in large refugee inflows into Chad. Refugees and internally displaced persons (IDPs) have increased threefold since 2014 (figure 1.3). As of December 2020, about 480,000 refugees were settled in 19 camps in the east, south, and Lake Chad regions (UNHCR 2020). In the east, about 324,000 Sudanese refugees are settled along the border (many for more than a decade), having fled violence in Darfur. In the south, Chad hosts about 99,000 refugees from the Central African Republic, the majority of whom have been in exile for more than a decade. In Lake Chad, some 20,000 Nigerian refugees who fled Boko Haram and intracommunal violence now reside near Chad's western border with Nigeria, Niger, and Cameroon. Women make up more than 55.5 percent of the refugee and IDP population, of whom 33.6 percent are of childbearing age. In addition, more than 208,000 IDPs are in the Lake Chad region.

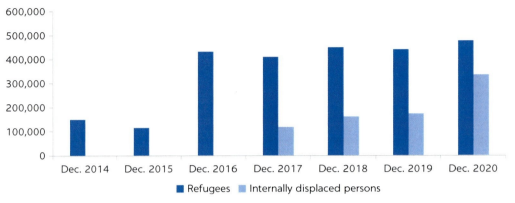

FIGURE 1.3
Refugees and internally displaced persons in Chad, 2014–20

Source: https://reporting.unhcr.org/chad-funding-2022.

Climate change is a multiplier of Chad's internal fragilities and conflicts. Climate variations directly affect agriculture and livestock, which account for 30 percent of the country's gross domestic product (GDP) and employ 80 percent of its workforce. Extreme rainfall, droughts, and floods negatively affect Chad's crop production and threaten food security.[1] The country has been particularly affected by global warming, given its position in the Sahel region. Since 2015, rainy seasons have become increasingly short, creating serious food security challenges. Furthermore, historical inter- and intracommunal conflicts, particularly those between pastoralists and agriculturalists, are exacerbated by changing transhumance flows and competition over scarce natural resources.

GDP per capita increased by more than 100 percent between 2000 and 2015, before it declined significantly between 2015 and 2020. GDP per capita (constant 2017 US$) increased from US$483 (US$939 purchasing power parity [PPP]) in 2000 to US$961 (US$1,866) in 2014, before falling to US$813 (US$1,579) in 2019 (figure 1.4). This period was characterized by an initial major positive shock—the onset of oil production—and the beginning of the oil super cycle. It allowed Chad to boost GDP per capita (PPP) from US$1,007 in 2002 to US$1,618 by 2005, rapidly distancing itself from other low-income countries and reducing the large income gap with the rest of SSA (figure 1.5). In 2019, GDP per capita (PPP) dropped to US$1,579 due to oil price shocks and renewed insecurity. Chad's continued reliance on oil has left the economy less diversified, less competitive, and more vulnerable to exogenous shocks.

Macroeconomic developments have followed the oil price dynamic. The oil price shock in 2014–15 led to a recession between 2016 and 2017. The economic recovery started in 2018 and continued in 2019 due to an increase in oil production and a significant recovery of the non-oil sector. However, the COVID-19 pandemic and the related decline in oil prices resulted in the economy contracting by 0.9 percent in 2020 (figure 1.6). The recession was less pronounced in Chad than in other oil-exporting countries in the Gulf of Guinea, thanks to previous investment in the oil sector that led to new fields coming onstream, the relatively low health impact of the pandemic, and the large share of the primary sector (which has been less impacted by the pandemic) in Chad's economy.

Containment measures have worsened the economic recession. The COVID-19 pandemic, with its worldwide containment measures, led to both regional and global supply and demand shocks, which have negatively affected

FIGURE 1.4
GDP per capita trends, 2014–20
Constant 2017 international dollars

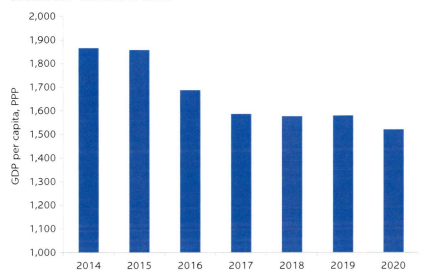

Source: World Development Indicators, https://data.worldbank.org/indicator.
Note: GDP = gross domestic product; PPP = purchasing power parity.

FIGURE 1.5
GDP per capita, PPP, 2000–20
Constant 2017 international dollars

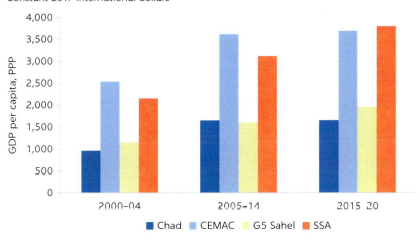

Source: World Development Indicators, https://data.worldbank.org/indicator.
Note: CEMAC = Economic and Monetary Community of Central Africa (Communauté Économique et Monétaire de l'Afrique Centrale); G5 Sahel = Burkina Faso, Chad, Mali, Mauritania, and Niger; PPP = purchasing power parity; SSA = Sub-Saharan Africa.

Chad's economy. After relaxing containment measures between August and October 2020, the authorities reintroduced some measures in the last two months of 2020 and in January 2021. The economy remained in recession in the first half of 2021, due to continued containment measures, public finance liquidity constraints (due to lower oil revenues and a decrease in grants), and economic disruption brought about by renewed armed conflict (which led to the death of President Idriss Déby Itno on April 20, 2021).

Chad continues to experience severe shortcomings in human development. It ranked 187th out of 189 countries in the United Nations Development Programme's 2020 *Human Development Report*, with a score of 0.401, only

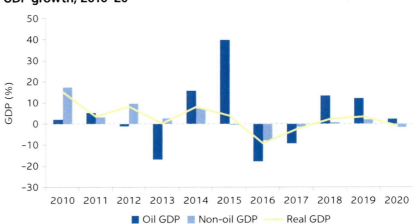

FIGURE 1.6
GDP growth, 2010–20

Sources: Chadian authorities and World Bank staff estimates.

higher than the Central African Republic and Niger. Life expectancy in Chad is estimated at 54 years, lower than in comparator countries and the SSA average (61 years in 2017). The average number of years of education for the population ages 25 years and older is only 2.4 years—only higher than Burkina Faso—while the expected years of schooling, which reflect current enrollment rates, are lower in Chad than in all benchmark countries. Poverty, displacement, and frequent episodes of insecurity make it difficult for families to invest in their human capital.

The country has, however, made some progress in education in recent years. The net primary enrollment rate has increased due to government programs aimed at strengthening the education system and building national capacity. For example, the National Education for All Action Plan was designed to improve the quality of human resources in the education system and integrate the network of schools in refugee camps into the national school system, among other objectives. The government has also improved access to learning by offering contracts to community teachers, who represent approximately 54 percent of teachers in Chad. These efforts helped to increase the net primary enrollment rate from 44.0 percent in 2011 to 73.2 percent in 2016, outperforming some neighboring countries, such as Mali (61.3 percent) and Niger (65.1 percent).[2]

POVERTY TRENDS

Poverty has been falling over the past decade

Poverty has been falling over the past decade, but it is estimated to have increased in 2020. While Chad has seen a progressive decline in monetary poverty since 2003, progress has slowed in recent years. ECOSIT survey data show that the proportion of the population living below the national poverty line declined from 54.8 percent in 2003 to 42.0 percent in 2018 (figure 1. 7). Not only did the share of the population living in poverty decrease, so did the depth and severity of poverty; those who remained in poverty got closer to the poverty line, and inequality between the poor declined. The reduction of poverty was larger in rural than urban areas, but poverty fell faster in both areas between 2003 and 2011 than after.

FIGURE 1.7
Trends in national poverty measures, 2003, 2011, and 2018

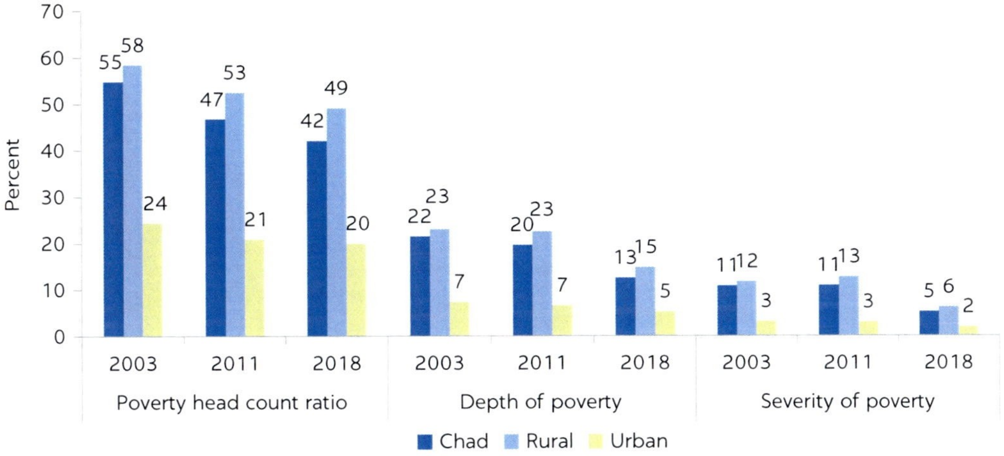

Sources: Chad INSEED 2011, 2018 (ECOSIT 3 and ECOSIT 4), and World Bank 2020.

The decline in poverty between 2011 and 2018 was driven by improvements in asset endowments and returns among poor households. Better access to employment opportunities led to an increase in nonfarm self-employment and an expansion of cellphone ownership. Coupled with an increase in the productive use of cellphones, this has increased household income and consumption, contributing to poverty reduction. To a lesser extent, wealthy and middle-class households also benefited from gains in the returns to motor-vehicle ownership.

Poverty has declined more slowly than population growth, resulting in an increase in the absolute number of poor Chadians. From 2011 to 2018, the population increased by more than 25 percent, while poverty declined by only 10 percent, resulting in an increase in the absolute number of poor people from 4.7 million to 6.5 million (figure 1.8). The increase was faster in urban areas, particularly in N'Djamena, where the population almost doubled and where the incidence of poverty increased slightly. However, in absolute terms, the number of poor people increased significantly in rural areas. In 2018, more than 88 percent of the poor (5.8 million) lived in rural areas, 0.7 million in urban areas, and 2.4 million were unable to meet the basic nutritional requirement (World Bank 2021).

Multidimensional poverty[3] has declined, along with monetary poverty (figure 1.9 and figure 1.10), but remains prevalent. Despite a 16 percent reduction since 2003, it remains high, fueled by limited access to education, electricity, and improved housing. All regions experienced a decline in multidimensional poverty in 2003–18, albeit at varying rates. The greatest decline was recorded in N'Djamena, where the rate of multidimensional poverty fell by 23 percentage points between 2003 and 2018, while it only fell by 3 percentage points in the regions of Guera and Salamat during the same period.

The decline in multidimensional poverty reflected significant progress in improving housing conditions, asset ownership, nutrition, education, and access to basic services among the country's poorest households. Increased cellphone ownership over the past 15 years and improvements in the material quality of housing have bolstered living standards. While the poor population continues to experience low indicators related to schooling and nutrition, pro-poor nutrition and education policies implemented over the years have contributed to some

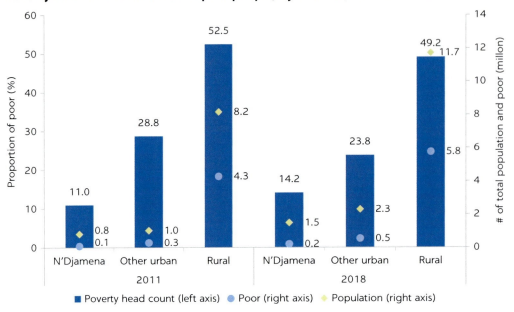

FIGURE 1.8
Poverty incidence and number of poor people, by location, 2011 and 2018

Sources: Chad INSEED 2011, 2018 (ECOSIT 3 and ECOSIT 4), and World Bank 2020.

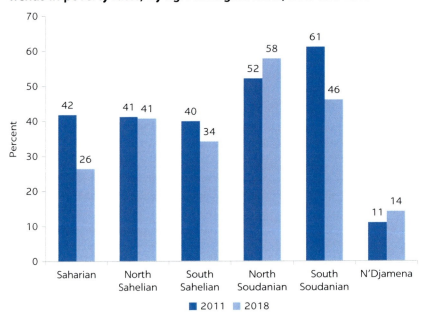

FIGURE 1.9
Trends in poverty rates, by agroecological zone, 2011 and 2018

Sources: Chad INSEED 2011, 2018 (ECOSIT 3 and ECOSIT 4).

improvements in these indicators as well. Moreover, improvements in access to services, such as electricity access in N'Djamena, have contributed to decreasing urban poverty. Access to improved water increased from 35 percent in 2011 to 55 percent in 2018, which has enabled women to spend less time on domestic activities and increased their engagement in nonfarm economic activities.

The COVID-19 pandemic threatens to reverse progress made in poverty reduction over the past decade. Disruptions in supply chains and commercial

FIGURE 1.10
Trends in poverty rates, by region, 2011 and 2018

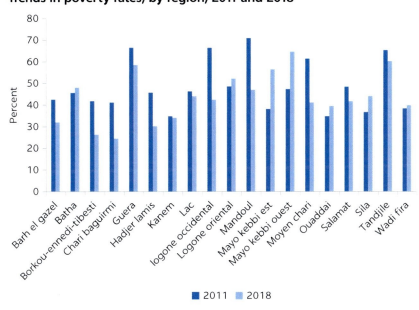

Sources: Chad INSEED 2011, 2018 (ECOSIT 3 and ECOSIT 4).

activities due to the pandemic have had an impact on employment and income levels, and the government's fiscal policies and social protection systems have been unable to fully offset these effects. Estimates indicate that the impact of the COVID-19 crisis on employment, remittances, and inflation increased the national poverty rate by as much as 5.5 percentage points in 2020—equivalent to an additional 849,574 people falling below the poverty line.

The geographic disparity in poverty is substantial

The spatial distribution of poverty shows a clear divergence between regions (map 1.1). Monetary poverty rates vary widely across regions and are especially high in rural areas and areas affected by conflict. About 88 percent of poor households live in rural areas, where the vast majority (89 percent) are engaged in agriculture. Agricultural households are particularly vulnerable because they are more likely than urban households to engage in low-yield agricultural activities and be exposed to price and climate shocks. The fall in the global price of cotton led to higher poverty rates in the country's cotton-growing areas, which include Logone Oriental and Sila. Mayo Kebbi, Tandjile, and Guera, where more than 90 percent of the population works in agriculture, had poverty rates above 60 percent in 2018. Areas that are particularly affected by climate change, and that have experienced prolonged dry seasons and lower rainfall (including Kanem, Barh El Ghazal, and Wadi Fira), have seen agricultural yields fall by up to 20 percent and continue to suffer from a high prevalence of poverty. Areas that share a border with the Central African Republic, Sudan, and Nigeria also have high poverty rates and are home to thousands of refugees fleeing violence and conflict. The highest rates of multidimensional poverty have been recorded in the country's Sahel region, where seven out of ten people in the regions of Batha, Sila, and Lac experience multidimensional poverty (map 1.2). While these are not the same regions that recorded the highest poverty head count ratios, their poverty rates were above the median.

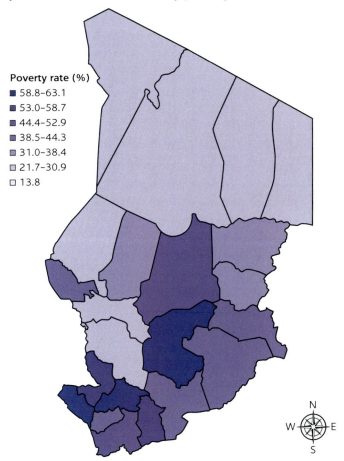

MAP 1.1
Geographic distribution of monetary poverty head count ratio, 2018

Poverty rate (%)
- 58.8–63.1
- 53.0–58.7
- 44.4–52.9
- 38.5–44.3
- 31.0–38.4
- 21.7–30.9
- 13.8

Sources: Chad INSEED 2018 (ECOSIT 4) and World Bank 2020.

The regional variation in poverty is amplified by geographic disparities in market access and connectivity. Poverty is concentrated in rural and isolated areas, where access to public services and connectivity to the rest of the country are quite limited. An analysis of market access indicates that a large portion of the population lives more than an hour's drive from the nearest market. This geographic distance is compounded by a lack of private vehicle ownership and limited public transit options. There is significant overlap between regions with poor market access and those with high rates of multidimensional poverty. Furthermore, public service delivery is hindered by severe infrastructure constraints: many roads lack proper maintenance, while others are vulnerable to insecurity. Improving the capacity of local governments to deliver goods and services in rural areas, which will significantly contribute to poverty reduction, will require complementary improvements in infrastructure, transportation, connectivity, and security.

The wide spatial disparity in poverty is a key factor influencing domestic migration, acting both as a motivation for migrating and as a barrier to mobility. As of 2018, 42 percent of the working-age population had migrated at some point in their lives. Welfare status influences migration decisions, with a higher percentage of nonpoor than poor working-age individuals migrating domestically. The lower rates of poverty among migrants may point to the economic benefits

MAP 1.2
Geographic distribution of multidimensional poverty index (MPI), 2018

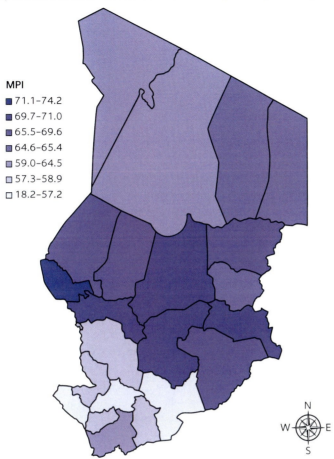

Sources: Chad INSEED 2018 (ECOSIT 4) and World Bank 2020.

of migration, but they are also influenced by selection bias: poverty itself may prevent some individuals from migrating.

Chad's migration phenomenon does not accelerate urbanization. The country's urbanization rate is very low compared to the SSA average and has remained broadly unchanged for 25 years. Indeed, poor migrants disproportionately migrate from rural areas to other rural communities: 74 percent of poor migrants were previously located in rural areas, of which 87 percent ended up in another rural location. Only 4 percent of poor migrants originating in rural communities move to N'Djamena, and 9 percent move to other urban areas. Nonpoor migrants, however, demonstrate greater mobility: those in rural communities still disproportionately migrate to other rural areas, but at a lower rate than their poor counterparts. A larger proportion of nonpoor migrants move to N'Djamena: 16 percent of those who originated in rural areas and 27 percent of those who originated in other urban areas. Variations in migration patterns between poor and nonpoor households are likely influenced by the unique barriers to migration experienced by the poor. While poor individuals may be less able to migrate due to financial constraints, they potentially stand to benefit more from migration, particularly if they move from rural to urban areas. In Chad, poor people migrate to follow their parents (24 percent), rejoin their family (21 percent), get married (33 percent), look for better opportunities (7 percent), or get access to land (2 percent). Yet, migration from rural areas is likely impeded by poor transportation networks, limited access to motor vehicles or public transport services, and high transports costs due to the aging vehicle fleet and damages incurred from the deteriorated road network.

NONMONETARY POVERTY

Access to education

Chad has made progress in expanding access to primary education, but gender disparities in access continue to persist. The net primary enrollment rate rose from 62 percent in 2011 to 73 percent in 2016, with the increase slightly higher for girls (47 to 64 percent) than boys (68 to 82 percent). Despite progress in expanding access to education for girls, primary enrollment rates are still far from equitable, with the country having the biggest gender gap in enrollment across all comparator countries (figure 1.11). The country's performance on the Gender Parity Index (GPI) for primary (0.77) and secondary (0.46) enrollment is the lowest among comparators.

Primary school completion rates continue to be low in Chad, driven by internal inefficiency and exacerbated by COVID-19. Rates of persistence to the last grade of primary education are the lowest among comparator countries, with fewer than one-third of students who enter the first year of primary school estimated to reach the last year. The repetition rate is 17 percent for both girls and boys, while the dropout rate is 33 percent for girls and 29 percent for boys.[4] Moreover, the number of children who drop out in primary school is almost twice as high as that in secondary school (725,795 in primary versus 383,093 for secondary school). This is in addition to 48 percent of primary school age children (47 percent for boys and 51 percent for girls) who had never attended school, yielding a rate of out-of-school children of 52 percent. The country has

FIGURE 1.11

Gross primary enrollment, 2003, 2015, and 2018

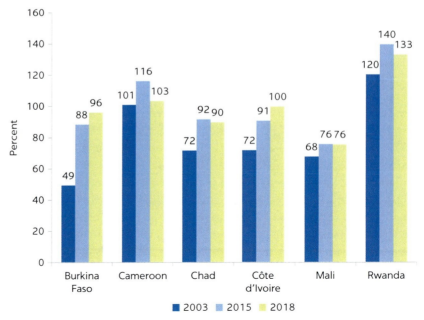

Source: World Development Indicators, https://data.worldbank.org/indicator.

made some progress in improving the quality of education since 2015, with the primary completion rate increasing from 29.7 percent in 2015 to 33.7 percent in 2018. However, Chad's primary completion rate remains relatively low compared to some comparator countries such as Burkina Faso, where it is almost twice as high. The closure of schools during the COVID-19 outbreak has increased the risk of dropping out of school, which in turn reduces human capital accumulation and the increases the risk of child marriage.

Secondary and tertiary enrollment rates have been increasing in recent years but remain low, especially for girls. Chad has made progress in improving access to secondary education, with the gross secondary enrollment rate rising from 14.8 percent in 2003 to close to 20.2 percent in 2018, with the rate more than doubling for girls (7 to 14 percent) and increasing for boys (22 to 26 percent). However, the country's secondary enrollment rate is still far below that of comparator countries (figure 1.12), and its gross tertiary enrollment rate remains very low (3 percent), driven mostly by male enrollment (5 percent, compared to the female enrollment rate of 1.5 percent) (figure 1.13).

Registration fees, contributions, and the cost of school supplies, uniforms, food, and transportation are some of the direct costs of education borne by students and their families. Among primary and secondary school-aged children, a lack of means to pay for education is the most cited reason for nonattendance, followed by dropping out due to failing grades (figure 1.14). Among children ages 6–17, 26 percent cite the cost of schooling or the lack of money to pay for education as the reason for not attending school. Although the lack of means to pay for education is the most cited reason across regions, it is particularly common in N'Djamena, where more than half of primary and secondary school-aged children cite this as their main reason for nonattendance. Dropouts due to failure is the second-most cited reason for nonattendance, both at the national level (21 percent) and across regions, although a slightly higher proportion of children in urban areas outside N'Djamena cite this as their primary reason (27 percent) (figure 1.15).

Chadian students who complete primary school have low absolute and relative levels of learning. Using the learning poverty metric,[5] nearly 94 percent of

FIGURE 1.12
Net secondary enrollment, 2018

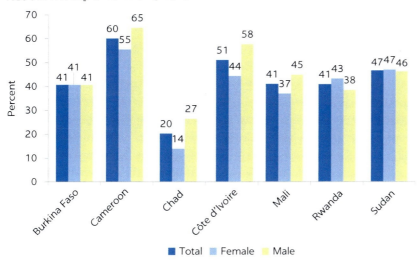

Source: World Development Indicators, https://data.worldbank.org/indicator.
Note: The most recent figures for Cameroon are from 2016 and for Sudan are from 2017.

FIGURE 1.13
Gross tertiary enrollment, 2017

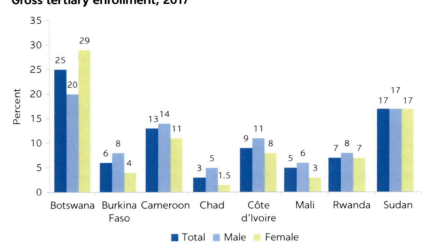

Source: World Development Indicators, https://data.worldbank.org/indicator.
Note: The most recent figures for Chad and Sudan are from 2015.

FIGURE 1.14
Reasons for not attending school, children ages 6–17, 2018

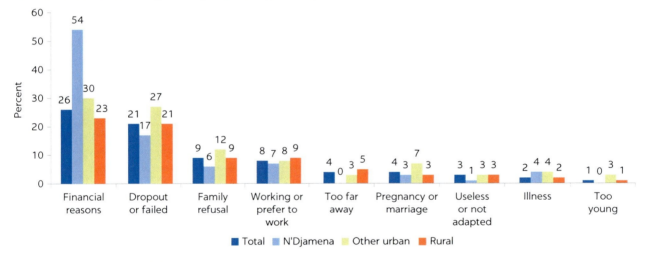

Source: Chad INSEED 2018 (ECOSIT 4).

Chadian children are failing in reading. This is higher than in SSA (by 11 percentage points) and other low-income countries (by 8 percentage points). At the end of primary school, Chadian students are poorly educated compared to the average of all peers on international evaluations in reading (22 percent of pupils at a satisfactory level versus 48 percent) and mathematics (12 percent versus 38 percent).[6] There is no significant gender differential. The overall situation did not evolve significantly between 2014 and 2019. Learning outcomes are markedly higher in urban than rural schools, and among children in the highest socioeconomic bracket.

The gender gaps in access to education are underpinned by social norms that appear to favor investments in boys' education and emphasize young women's reproductive role over their income-generating role as they approach adolescence. The proportion of children of primary and secondary school age who cite family refusal as their primary reason of nonattendance is more than double for

FIGURE 1.15
Reasons for not attending school, girls ages 14–19, 2018

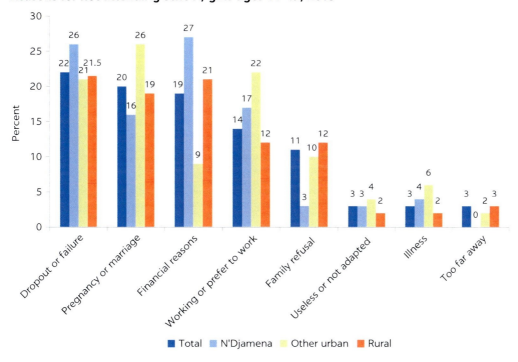

Source: Chad INSEED 2018 (ECOSIT 4).

girls (11.9 percent) compared to boys (5.6 percent), with wide variation across regions. Family refusal presents a bigger challenge in urban areas outside N'Djamena—where more than 17 percent of girls ages 6–17 years old cite it for nonattendance, much higher than 3 percent of boys—and rural areas—where 11 percent of girls cite this as a reason for nonattendance, compared to 6 percent of boys. Although the share of girls who cite family refusal as a reason for not attending school is relatively lower in N'Djamena (10 percent, compared to 1 percent of boys), it still presents a challenge.

Access to health care

Despite improvements in key health outcomes in recent years, trends indicate continued slow progress toward achieving the Sustainable Development Goals (SDGs). The maternal mortality rate fell from 1,450 per 100,000 live births in 1990 to 1,140 in 2017—still far from the SDG target of 70 by 2030. In addition, the under-five mortality rate fell from 213 per 1,000 live births in 1990 to 131 in 2015 and 71 in 2018—compared to the SDG target of 25 by 2030. In 2018 Chad had the third-highest under-five mortality rate in the world. Moreover, Chad's mortality rate remains high relative to the average of low-income countries, SSA, and the Economic and Monetary Community of Central Africa (CEMAC). The country's health outcomes are largely explained by the combination of a poorly performing health sector and broad development challenges such as demographic trends and social determinants of health.

High maternal mortality and fertility rates indicate a need for better access to health care services and higher quality of care, especially in terms of reproductive health. With 5.7 births per woman in 2018, which is a slight decrease from

6.5 births per woman in 2011, Chad has one of the highest fertility rates among comparator countries, second only to Mali (5.9 births per woman) and higher than the average for SSA (4.8 births per woman) (figure 1.16.a).[7] The high fertility rate adds further pressure on the country's health care system. High fertility rates are closely linked to high maternal and infant mortality rates. This is mainly explained by the low coverage of reproductive and maternal health services, which could contribute to longer spacing between births and help identify high-risk pregnancies. Despite progress over the past decade, the rate of births attended by skilled health care personnel is far lower in Chad than in benchmark countries (figure 1.16.b). Demographic and Health Survey data reveal that postnatal care for both mothers and infants is also particularly low in Chad, with 78 percent of mothers and most newborns (94 percent) not receiving postnatal care within 41 days of birth (Chad INSEED, MSP, and ICF 2016). These critical gaps in service delivery result in maternal mortality rates far higher than those of comparator countries (figure 1.16.c).

While slight improvements have been recorded, Chad performs worse on child health indicators than its peers. Rates of stunting in children increased from 39 to 40 percent in 2010–15. Moreover, Chad still has the highest rate of wasting among all comparator countries, and it only performs better than Sudan on indicators of underweight and stunting. Vaccination rates are also generally low in Chad and vary widely across regions and based on the educational attainment of the mother. Demographic and Health Survey data (Chad INSEED, MSP, and ICF 2016) reveal that only a quarter of all children ages 12–23 months have received all prescribed vaccines, while 19 percent of children ages 12–23 months have yet to receive any vaccine. These gaps result in the highest under-five mortality rate among comparator countries, estimated at 119 deaths per 1,000 live births in 2018.

The country's poor performance in health outcomes can be attributed to the low coverage of essential health services. This in turn is due to the low readiness of health facilities to deliver quality care as well as the poor performance of community platforms to support health promotion and prevention activities. A lack of means to pay for health services keeps Chadians from seeking care. ECOSIT 4 data show that more than 61 percent of Chadians (57 percent in urban areas and 63 percent in rural areas) who experienced recent illness chose not to seek medical consultation. The most common reason for not seeking care, excluding self-medication, was the cost associated with health services, with 76 percent citing either the lack of finances to pay for health services or health care being too expensive. Distance to hospitals and health centers can also pose a challenge to accessing care, especially in rural areas. Ten percent of people living in rural areas with recent illnesses did not seek care because of the distance to health centers, while only 1.4 percent of residents of N'Djamena and 3 percent of urban residents cite this as a reason for not seeking care.

The COVID-19 crisis severely affected the population's well-being, and it has caused significant disruptions in health service delivery. For instance, routine immunization campaigns were postponed, and significant resources were committed to preparing the health system to prevent the spread of the virus. Phone survey data show that among people who rated their well-being as difficult (the lowest in the scale), 65 percent indicated that their well-being had been adversely affected by COVID-19.

Increased ownership of mobile phones has also helped to reduce poverty. While Chadian households added few assets between 2011 and 2018, ownership

FIGURE 1.16
Maternal health and fertility rates

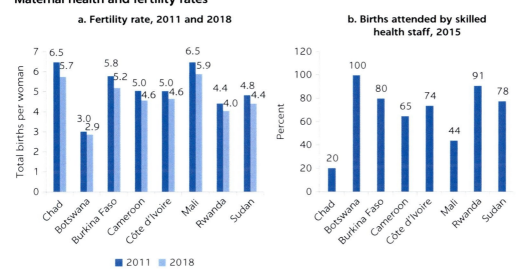

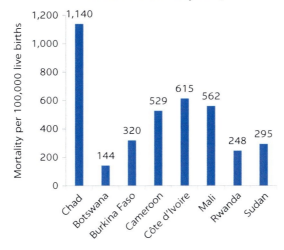

Sources: UNDP 2019 and World Development Indicators, https://data.worldbank.org/indicator.

of mobile phones rose considerably, especially among lower-income groups and urban households (figure 1.17). The rise in mobile phone ownership among rural and poor households was from a very low base and thus generated significant gains in consumption—both in terms of the endowment itself and the economic returns generated from the productive use of mobile phones. Meanwhile, ownership of more sophisticated communication and transportation assets (for example, computers, televisions, motorcycles, and cars) rose faster in urban and better-off households, which had little impact on poverty.

An increase in access to electricity and improved drinking water led to an increase in household consumption, but progress to improve access remains slow. Access to the electrical grid and the use of safe drinking water[8] have increased for both rural and urban households, but the increase in access to electricity has been significantly higher in N'Djamena than in the rest of the country, while the use of improved drinking water has been higher in rural than urban areas (figure 1.18). These improvements have contributed to poverty reduction,

FIGURE 1.17
Ownership of assets, 2011 and 2018

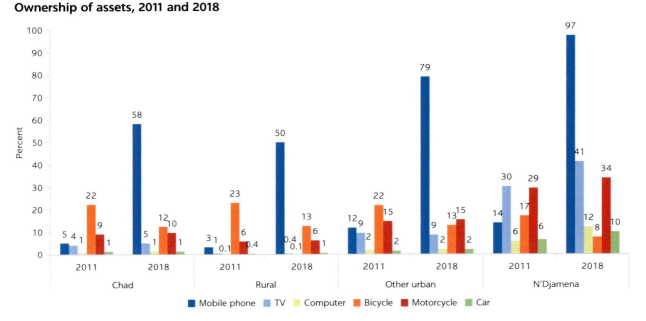

Sources: Chad INSEED 2011, 2018 (ECOSIT 3 and ECOSIT 4).

FIGURE 1.18
Access to basic services, by location, 2011 and 2018

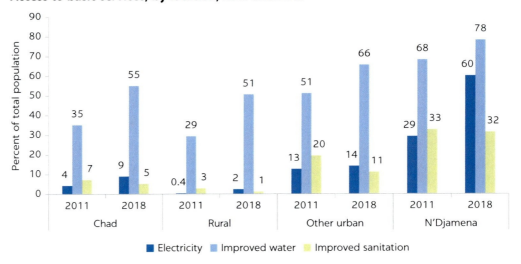

Sources: Chad INSEED 2011, 2018 (ECOSIT 3 and ECOSIT 4).

although most of the positive effects on the consumption of poor and vulnerable households have been in the capital city, while the impact on their consumption in rural areas has been marginal. Access to basic services remains very low: about 90 percent of households nationwide and almost the entire rural population lack access to the electrical grid; more than 40 percent of all households and 46 percent of rural households only have access to unsafe sources of drinking water; access to basic sanitation is still highly problematic, particularly in rural areas; and more than 90 percent of all households and more than 99 percent of rural households continue to rely on inefficient energy sources for cooking.

Access to basic infrastructure and services

The level of access to public services continues to be lower in Chad than in comparator countries. In 2018, a smaller proportion of Chad's population had access to electricity, basic sanitation, and basic drinking water than any of its comparator countries (figure 1.19). Due to the severe gaps in service delivery, the country had the greatest number of deaths attributed to unsafe water, unsafe sanitation, and lack of hygiene among comparators in 2016 (figure 1.20). For example, the mortality rate attributed to unsafe water, unsafe sanitation, and lack of hygiene in Chad is 1.4 times higher than in Mali, which has the second-highest mortality rate.

FIGURE 1.19
Access to basic services, Chad and comparator countries, 2017–18

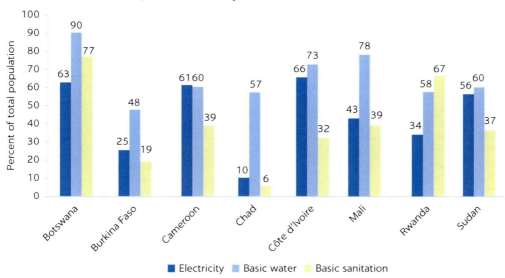

Sources: Chad INSEED 2018 (ECOSIT 4) and World Development Indicators, https://data.worldbank.org/indicator.
Note: Figures are percentages of total population. Data for Chad are from 2018 and for comparator countries from 2017.

FIGURE 1.20
Mortality rate attributed to unsafe water, unsafe sanitation, and lack of hygiene, 2016

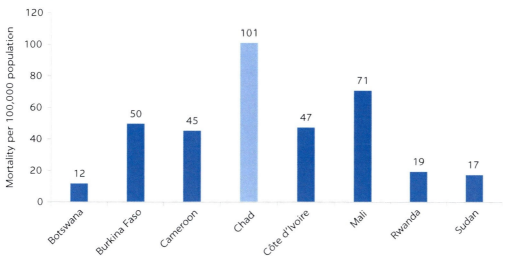

Source: World Development Indicators, https://data.worldbank.org/indicator.

INEQUALITY AND SHARED PROSPERITY

Inequality declined between 2011 and 2018, and signs of pro-poor growth have emerged. The consumption-based Gini coefficient fell from 42.1 percent in 2011 to 33.4 percent in 2018. Inequality fell across the board but faster in rural areas, where the Gini coefficient seems to have declined from 41.6 percent to 30.3 percent, compared with a decline from 36.2 percent to 33.6 percent in urban zones. The growth incidence curve for 2011–18, which shows the percent change in average consumption for each percentile of the distribution, is downwardly sloped, indicating higher growth among the poorest population groups (figure 1.21). This pattern is mainly observed in rural areas, while the pro-poor benefits were limited in urban areas, particularly in N'Djamena.

Large inequalities between households, driven by their demographic composition and the employment sector of the household head, suggest an opportunity to accelerate poverty reduction through faster demographic and economic transformation. In Chad, households in the bottom 40 percent of the consumption distribution are extremely poor, live in rural areas, and tend to have many children. Moreover, their head of household is less educated

FIGURE 1.21
Growth incidence curves, 2011–18

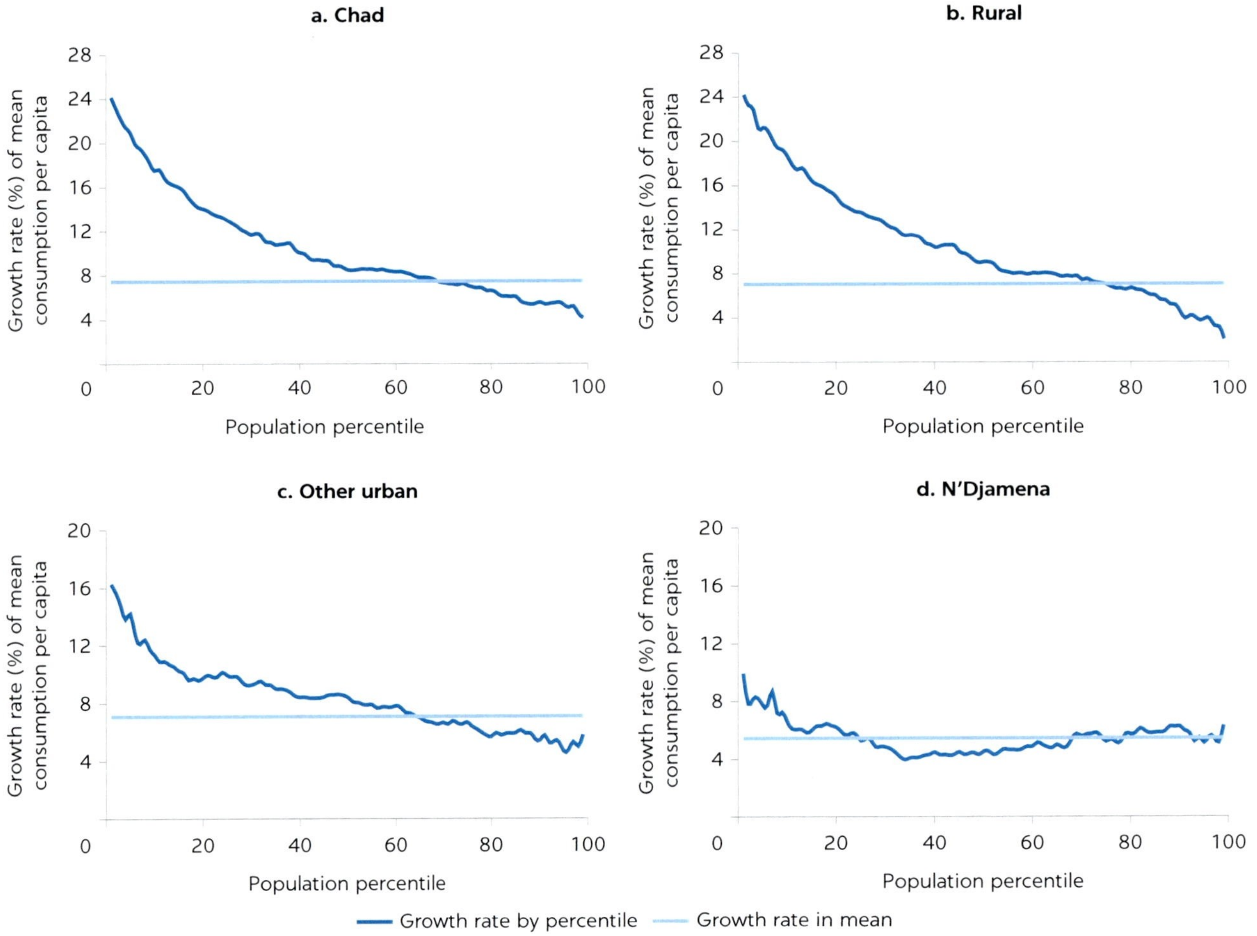

Sources: Chad INSEED 2011, 2018 (ECOSIT 3 and ECOSIT 4).

than the average household head and tends to be self-employed or work in agriculture. According to 2018 data, differences in household demographic composition (based on the number of children) account for about 18 percent of total inequality. The per capita consumption level of households with fewer than three children below age 15 is, on average, 1.8 times higher than that of households with 5 children or more.

This suggests that efforts to reduce the fertility rate and catalyze the demographic transition would contribute to an acceleration of poverty reduction. Similarly, differences between households due to the employment sector of the household head account for about 16 percent of total inequality. Households headed by someone who works in the services and industry sectors have average consumption levels about 1.7 times and 1.5 times higher, respectively, than households headed by a worker in agriculture, an indication that a faster transition of labor to more productive sectors (such as, services and industry) would foster income growth and poverty reduction. This transition should consider regional disparities, as high spatial inequalities can exacerbate social tensions and fragility and impede inclusive growth and shared prosperity. Indeed, differences between urban and rural areas account for about 14 percent of total inequality, and inequality between geographic locations accounts for about 10 percent.

The COVID-19 pandemic is expected to lead to an increase in inequality. Data from the first (May–June 2020) and third (January–February 2021) rounds of the high frequency survey show that the share of households from the lowest income quintile that lost a part of their total income increased by 10 percentage points during the six-month period, higher than the 3 percentage point increase for households in the highest quintile. The decline in households' total income was partly due to a reduction in the frequency and level of remittances, particularly for households in the poorest quintile. As a result, the disparity in income between rich and poor households is projected to continue to widen, leading to an increase in inequality.

LOW ACCESS TO EMPLOYMENT

Despite relatively high rates of employment, most workers are employed in low-skill occupations,[9] while youth constitute most of the country's unemployed and discouraged workers.[10] More than 73 percent of the country's total population ages 15 years and older are active in the labor force. Of the active population, only 0.92 percent are included in the International Labour Organization's strict definition of unemployment, which excludes discouraged workers. Including discouraged workers, the country's hidden unemployment rate increases to an estimated 2.6 percent, as the proportion of discouraged workers is much higher than the unemployed who are actively seeking work. Youth constitute most discouraged workers and the unemployed, which signals the lack of opportunities and the limited capacity of the private sector to absorb new entrants into the labor market.

Self-employment and jobs with relatively low productivity dominate employment in Chad. More than 90 percent of the employed population is either self-employed or employed by households, while employment in higher-skill occupations is exceedingly low—only an estimated 3 percent of the employed population works in managerial positions or as employers, and 1.7 percent works as skilled laborers (figure 1.22). The dominance of

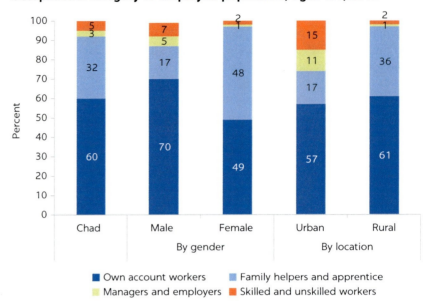

FIGURE 1.22
Occupational category of employed population, ages 15+, 2018

Source: Chad INSEED 2018 (ECOSIT 4).

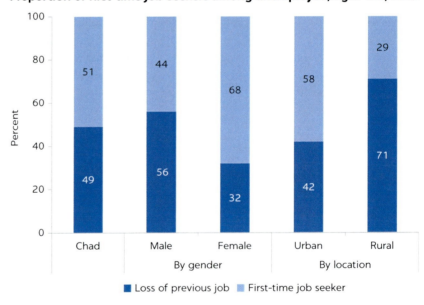

FIGURE 1.23
Proportion of first-time job seekers among unemployed, ages 15+, 2018

Source: Chad INSEED 2018 (ECOSIT 4).

employment in low-skill occupations is even more pronounced in rural areas, where more than 96 percent of the employed population are either self-employed or employed by households, while approximately 1 percent are skilled workers or managers. Employment in low-skill occupations is also more prevalent among women, driven by high rates of household work (48 percent) relative to their male peers (17 percent) (figure 1.23).

Low unemployment obscures relatively high rates of discouraged workers, most of whom are young. More than 60 percent of the unemployed are 30 years old and below, and more than half of the total unemployed are first-time job seekers, which underscores the challenges that youth face in finding employment. An estimated 75 percent of discouraged workers are between the ages of 15 to 30 years, of whom more than 22 percent have at least a lower secondary education.

The high proportion of youth among the unemployed and discouraged workers, along with the small size of the private sector, point to the challenges that the country could face in the years to come. The lack of employment opportunities available to Chadians is likely to be magnified in the future, given the country's young population. The country's working-age population is projected to double by 2045, which will exert even more pressure on the country's labor market.

NOTES

1. Data in this section are from the Climate Change Knowledge Portal (database), World Bank Group, Washington, DC (accessed June 9, 2020): https://climateknowledgeportal.worldbank.org/country/chad.
2. As a result, the country made slight progress in improving its HCI score, which increased from 0.29 in 2010 to 0.30 in 2020.
3. The Multidimensional Poverty Index measures deprivations across six categories: education, health, children and youth, access to basic services, housing conditions, and assets, and an individual is multidimensionally poor if deprived in at least two of the six dimensions. It was measured at 70 percent in 2003, 66 percent in 2011, and 59 percent in 2018.
4. The ECOSIT 4 survey reports the primary reasons are opportunity costs and lack of learning for boys and girls (who also are affected by social norms).
5. Learning poverty means being unable to read and understand a short, age-appropriate text by age 10. This indicator captures both the share of children who have not achieved minimum reading proficiency and the share of children who are out of school.
6. Programme d'Analyse des Systèmes Educatifs de la CONFEMEN (PASEC) international learning outcomes survey. PASEC 2019, http://www.pasec.confemen.org/.
7. The fertility rate for Niger is 6.9, but Niger is not considered a comparator country for Chad in this analysis.
8. Safe or improved drinking water refers to "basic water," as defined in the SDGs as drinking water from an improved water source located on premises (piped water) or a source (for example, tube wells, boreholes, protected dug wells, protected springs, and rainwater collection) that can be reached with no more than a 30-minute round trip.
9. This constraint was not prioritized in 2015 because the focus was on rural areas. However, COVID-19 led to containment measures that disproportionally affected the urban informal sector.
10. Individuals of working age who are available for work but do not seek it due to reasons related to the labor market, such as uncertainty regarding how to find work, past failure in seeking employment, or lack of experience.

REFERENCES

Chad INSEED (Tchad Institut National de la Statistique, des Études Économiques et Démographiques). 2011. *Tchad, Troisieme enquête sur la consommation et le secteur informel au Tchad-ECOSIT 3.*

Chad INSEED (Tchad, Institut National de la Statistique, des Études Économiques et Démographiques). 2018. *Tchad, Quatrieme enquête sur la consommation et le secteur informel au Tchad-ECOSIT 4.*

Chad INSEED, MSP, and ICF (Institut National de la Statistique, des Études Économiques et Démographiques [INSEED], Ministère de la Santé Publique [MSP], et ICF

International. 2016. "Enquête Démographique et de Santé et à Indicateurs Multiples au Tchad (EDS-MICS) 2014–2015)." ICF International: Rockville, Maryland, USA. https://dhsprogram.com/pubs/pdf/FR317/FR317.pdf.

Magrin, G. *2016.* "The Disappearance of Lake Chad: History of a Myth." *Journal of Political Ecology* 23 (1): 204–22.

UN DESA (United Nations Department of Economic and Social Affairs, Population Division). 2019. *World Population Prospects 2019, Volume II: Demographic Profiles.* ST/ESA/SER.A/427. https://population.un.org/wpp/Publications/Files/WPP2019_Volume-II-Demographic-Profiles.pdf.

UNDP (United Nations Development Programme). 2019. *Human Development Report 2019: Beyond Income, Beyond Averages, Beyond Today—Inequalities in Human Development in the 21st Century.* New York: UNDP. https://hdr.undp.org/content/human-development-report-2019.

UNDP (United Nations Development Programme). 2020. *Human Development Report 2020: The Next Frontier—Human Development and the Anthropocene.* New York: UNDP. https://hdr.undp.org/content/human-development-report-2020.

UNHCR (United Nations Refugee Agency). 2020. "UNHCR Sahel Crisis Response, 16–30 April 2020." External Operational Update. http://reporting.unhcr.org/sites/default/files/UNHCR%20Sahel%20Crisis%20Response%20-%20Operational%20Update%20-%2016-30%20April%202020.pdf.

World Bank. 2020. "Chad: Economic and Poverty Update under COVID-19, Spring 2020." World Bank, Washington, DC. https://openknowledge.worldbank.org/handle/10986/34563.

World Bank. 2021. "Chad Poverty Assessment: Investing in Rural Income Growth, Human Capital, and Resilience to Support Sustainable Poverty Reduction." World Bank, Washington, DC. https://openknowledge.worldbank.org/handle/10986/36443.

2 Binding Constraints on Poverty Reduction and Shared Prosperity

OVERVIEW

In 2021, Chad faced several binding constraints that negatively affect economic growth and inclusion. Some of these constraints—such as weak access to infrastructure, low agricultural productivity, and limited human capital accumulation—were already identified in the 2015 Systematic Country Diagnostic (SCD). However, other constraints have also emerged, such as increasing insecurity and climate change issues, challenges in managing oil revenue volatility, and low access to formal employment.

CONSTRAINTS IDENTIFIED IN 2015 THAT REMAIN

The 2015 SCD identified four major constraints to achieve the World Bank's twin goals of eliminating extreme poverty and boosting shared prosperity in Chad: (a) weak access to physical and human capital, (b) low social returns to economic activities in rural areas, (c) individual appropriation of returns to investment and entrepreneurship, and (d) lack of incentives and capacity among the authorities to address constraints to poverty reduction. This 2021 SCD Update presents these constraints and five other binding constraints that were not addressed in the 2015 SCD.

Weak access to infrastructure is due to insufficient and inefficient public investments

Access to basic infrastructure remains very low.[1] About 90 percent of households nationwide, along with almost the entire rural population, lack access to the electrical grid; more than 40 percent of households and 46 percent of rural households only have access to unsafe sources of drinking water; drinking water remains a tremendous challenge for rural and poor households; access to basic sanitation is still highly problematic, particularly in rural areas; and more than 90 percent of all households and more than 99 percent of rural households continue to rely on inefficient energy sources for cooking. In 2018, a smaller proportion of Chad's population had access to electricity, basic sanitation, and basic drinking water than any comparator country (figure 2.1). Due to these severe gaps in service delivery, the country had the greatest number of deaths attributed to unsafe water, unsafe sanitation, and lack of hygiene among comparators in 2016.

An increase in access to electricity and improved drinking water led to an increase in household consumption, but progress to improve access remains slow. Access to the electrical grid and the use of safe drinking water[2] have increased for both rural and urban households, but the increase in access to electricity has been significantly higher in N'Djamena than in the rest of the country, while the use of improved drinking water has increased much faster in rural than urban areas (figure 2.2). These improvements have contributed to poverty reduction, although most of the positive effects on the consumption of poor and vulnerable households have been in the capital city, while the impact on their consumption in rural areas has been marginal.

Chad is a global outlier in terms of energy access. Despite the endowment of fossil fuels and solar resources, Chad has one of the lowest electricity access rates in the world, estimated at 6.4 percent, with significant disparities between urban (20 percent) and rural (1 percent) areas. In a country with a population exceeding 16 million people and growing at more than 3 percent per year, the existing capacity of only about 170 MW, which is made of city-based isolated power islands, falls well short of the country's needs. Even people with access to electricity encounter daily interruptions in the power supply. The main issues facing the country's energy sector include deficient governance, inadequate tariffs, high production costs, and lack of policies to enable private investments in off-grid access (figure 2.3).

Public spending cuts have constrained investment in basic infrastructure. The level of public investment spending remains insufficient and dependent on

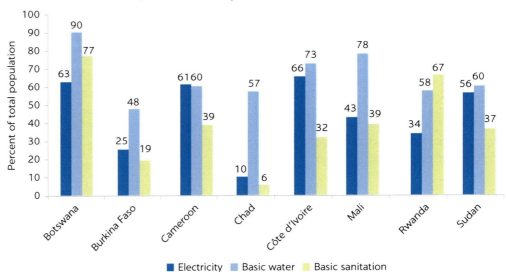

FIGURE 2.1
Access to basic services, Chad and comparator countries, 2017–18

Sources: Chad INSEED 2018 (ECOSIT 4) and World Development Indicators, https://data.worldbank.org/indicator.
Note: Figures are percentages of total population. Data for Chad are from 2018 and for comparator countries from 2017.

FIGURE 2.2
Access to basic services, by location, 2011 and 2018

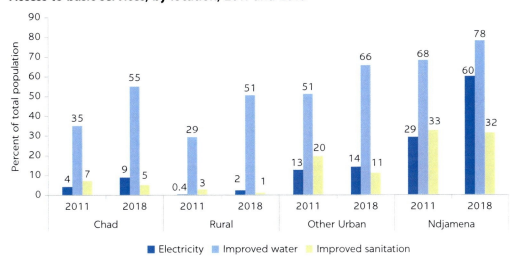

Sources: Chad INSEED 2011, 2018 (ECOSIT 3 and ECOSIT 4).

FIGURE 2.3
Main challenges facing the electricity sector in Chad

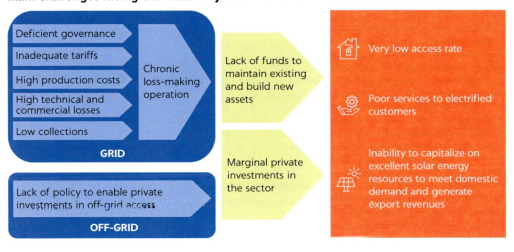

Source: World Bank.

external financing, creating a significant infrastructure gap and resulting in poor-quality infrastructure, particularly in rural areas. Public investment increased from 4.3 percent of GDP in 2019 to 6.8 percent of GDP in 2020. Between 2015 and 2020, the overall budget allocation for public investment in energy, transportation, telecommunications, and water averaged 28 percent of the country's total investment budget. The public investment budget was mainly dependent on external financing during this period (58 percent of externally financed public investment). As the current crisis is expected to have a considerable impact on Chad's public revenue over the next couple of years, investment spending and transfers are expected to rely strongly on external financing. Despite some recent improvement, significant efforts are still needed to increase the technical and allocative efficiency of public spending in Chad.

Weak productivity and exports reduce the return on agricultural and livestock activities

Households that earn their livelihood from agriculture, which suffers from low productivity and a high degree of exposure to shocks in Chad, are more likely to be poor.[3] In 2018, about 52 percent of households whose heads worked in agriculture were poor, highlighting the prevalence of subsistence agriculture in the country. By contrast, the poverty rate drops to 28 percent and 18 percent when the head of household works in industry and services, respectively. Approximately 68 percent of households own land that can be utilized for cultivation, and agriculture remains the main economic activity in rural areas. Agricultural land ownership[4] is characterized by relatively small land holdings, with 88 percent of land-owning households owning less than 5 hectares (ha) of land. Cultivation of crops is more common among poor households, and cereals are the most frequently cultivated crops. While poor households are more likely to own land than nonpoor households, their land holdings tend to be slightly smaller than the average. Nevertheless, the country has significant agricultural potential, with total cultivable land estimated at 39 million ha, of which 5.6 million ha are irrigable and 435,000 ha (including 100,000 ha of oasis agriculture land) are easy to develop. However, any such effort would need to take into account the significant and growing intra- and intercommunal tensions and conflicts among farmers and pastoralists, as well as within these socioeconomic groups, around access to natural resources (for example, land and water), including the governance and economic interests linked to these resources. About 4.5 million ha of land, on average, was cultivated annually over the past 5 years (less than 12 percent of the potential), of which two-thirds were in the Sahelian zone and one-third in the Sudanian zone. While land is available to increase areas under cultivation and augment agricultural production, the tools and means to exploit and irrigate land arrears are lacking.

A combination of factors reduces productivity in the agriculture sector. These include (a) the risky and variable production environment; (b) a lack of effective public investment, extension services, and postbasic skills, which are associated with the limited uptake of new technologies; (c) a lack of improved water and land management, which hampers efforts to increase yields and reduce climate-related risks; (d) a lack of up- and downstream value-chain integration; (e) limited connectivity to local and international markets; and (f) insecure land tenure.

Despite Chad's high potential in livestock production, several constraints prevent the sector from reaching its production and trade potential. The livestock sector represents about one-fourth of value added in the agriculture sector, supports about 40 percent of the rural population, and contributes substantially to the country's food security through the production of meat (slaughter), milk, and eggs, as well as through the associated household income. Beyond livestock, several other breeding activities are significant sources of income for rural households, such as poultry farming, nonconventional breeding, beekeeping, and so on. However, the constraints to developing the sector range from sanitary issues at the production level to challenges related to transport and border crossings as well as the high prevalence of informality. The multiplicity of intermediaries in the export value chain also significantly reduces the share of income for breeders and small-scale producers. Other key constraints include logistical challenges, clearance delays due to lack of agency coordination and extensive paperwork, and congestion at border points. Longer waiting times often lead to a reduction in animal weight, and delays undermine the norms and standards in the trading of meat, causing livestock or products to be either rejected on arrival or sold at significantly reduced prices.

Weak access to education and health care is due to insufficient and inefficient public financing

With an average population growth rate estimated at 3.3 percent, the country's education and training system is facing substantial demographic pressure.[5] According to estimates based on the 2009 census, 56 percent (8.6 million) of the population is between 3 and 24 years old, and this group is estimated to reach 13.5 million by 2030. Moreover, the share of the primary school–age population (ages 6–11 years) in the overall population was 18 percent in 2018, which is expected to be maintained (or even slightly increase) until 2030. As a result, the country's demographic constraints are relatively severe.

However, education spending as a share of government spending remains low and significantly below the Global Partnership for Education (GPE) standard. The share of education in total public expenditures decreased from 15.4 percent in 2013 to 8.9 percent in 2015, recovered and increased to 11.0 percent in 2019, before falling to 9.5 percent in 2020 (significantly lower than the GPE standard of 20 percent). Education does not appear to be treated as a priority in Chad, as the share of education in total public expenditures tends to be reduced in the event of a shock or crisis. The 2019 Public Expenditure Review (PER) for Chad shows that the share of public spending on education as a percentage GDP has remained less than 3 percent in recent years. Moreover, funding for education increased to 14 percent of the public budget in 2017, before dropping drastically to 10 percent in 2018 and setting at 12 percent in 2019. The main source of funding for public and community schools is the contribution from parents (45 percent), and only 3 in 10 teachers in primary education are paid by the government. The distribution of teachers differs widely across the country, with a strong concentration of teachers in N'Djamena.

The poor performance of education and training in Chad reflects not only inadequate public spending but also inefficient education expenditures. The country's education system is internally inefficient and is characterized by an inadequate quality of teaching. Peer countries allocate about 2–3 percent of GDP to education but have a much higher school life expectancy than Chad. These include Cameroon, the Democratic Republic of Congo, and Madagascar, which invest 2.8, 2.2, and 3.0 percent of GDP, respectively, in education and have attained a school life expectancy of 11.5, 9.3, and 10.2 years, respectively. This shows that despite the low level of education funding, it is possible for Chad to increase the efficient use of resources and achieve higher levels of schooling. The primary school dropout rate increased from 10 percent in 2013 to 20 percent in 2016. Between 2011 and 2016, the average repetition rate in primary education was about 23 percent—higher than the average for peer countries. The cost of this inefficiency is estimated to be 0.3 percent of GDP in 2018. This represented 59 percent of primary education resources in 2016 (UNESCO 2016).

The health sector remains labor intensive, with insufficient qualified health personnel affecting the adequate delivery of health care. According to the National Health Development Plan 2017–21, Chad's Ministry of Public Health had 8,149 health personnel at the end of 2016 (Chad Santé 2018). The density of health personnel at the national level was estimated at 0.58 per 1,000 inhabitants in 2016—much lower than the standard recommended to achieve the SDGs by the WHO of 4.45 per 1,000 inhabitants. At the regional level, 18 out of 23 provinces have a density of less than 0.6 health personnel per 1,000 inhabitants. Only the provinces of Tibesti-Est, Ennedi-Ouest, and N'Djamena have relatively high densities of 5.57, 1.49, and 3.05, respectively. While the high densities in the two provinces in the extreme north are explained by their relatively low populations, N'Djamena has about 46 percent of the total number of health personnel while representing only 9 percent of the total population.

The country's slow progress in improving the health sector reflects inadequate and insufficient public health expenditures relative to both regional and structural comparators. According to the WHO National Health Accounts database, Chad's health expenditures totaled CFAF 272 billion (4.5 percent of GDP) in 2016, lower than the average of SSA (5.1 percent of GDP) and lower-income countries (LICs) (5.7 percent). In per capita terms, Chad spends US$32 per inhabitant, much lower than the SSA and LIC averages of US$82 and US$35, respectively. Among structural peers, Chad only performs better than the Democratic Republic of Congo (US$21). The country's weak health expenditures also reflect challenges in the supply of medical products. Current health expenditures are calculated as the unit price (cost) multiplied by the quantities of goods and services used. Since the price of medical goods and services is usually high (see Chad Santé 2018), low health expenditures imply low availability of medical goods and services.[6] Chad's health system is largely financed by direct payments from households, as household spending accounts for more than 61 percent of current health expenditures, followed by government spending (19 percent) and external sources (15 percent).

Low inclusion of women in the economy and slow demographic transition

Poverty is correlated with the number of children and other dependents in the household.[7] In 2018/19, poor households had 1.4 times more children ages 15 years and younger than nonpoor households, resulting in a higher dependency rate for poor households (2.1) compared with their nonpoor counterparts (1.5). Approximately 58 percent of households with five or more children younger than 15 are poor, 4.5 times as high as the poverty rate for households with no children (estimated at 13 percent), 16 percentage points higher than the national average poverty rate, and 33 percentage points higher than the poverty rate for households with one or two children (figure 2.4).

Poverty also seems to be more prevalent among women. Although household surveys assume equal distribution of consumption between members of a household, there are indications that poverty is more prevalent among women, particularly in urban areas, where the poverty rate is 24 percent for female-headed households, higher than 19 percent for male-headed households (figure 2.5). Some types of women-headed households are particularly vulnerable to poverty, and married women in polygamous households are significantly poorer than the rest of the population. Ownership of assets, especially transportation and communication equipment, is also significantly lower in female-headed households, which illustrates the limited access of women to productive assets.

According to the 2021 Chad Gender Report, gender gaps in school attendance are narrowing, but girls still have lower educational attainment and poorer learning outcomes than boys (World Bank 2021a). Moreover, women constitute half of Chad's working population but are less productive and earn less than men.

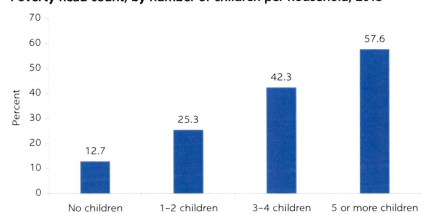

FIGURE 2.4
Poverty head count, by number of children per household, 2018

Source: Chad INSEED 2018 (ECOSIT 4).

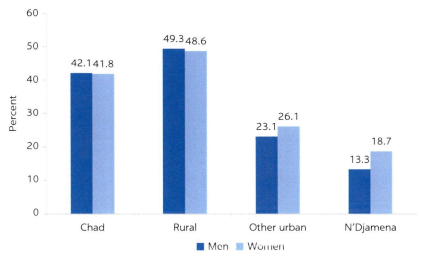

FIGURE 2.5
Poverty head count, by gender of household head, 2018

Source: Chad INSEED 2018 (ECOSIT 4).

Only 50 percent of women participate in the labor force, lower than 73 percent of men.[8] Moreover, women are less likely to join the formal labor force and work for pay, and they do not have access to the same work opportunities as men. And even when they do, women are more likely to work part time or in the informal sector. Time use constraints for women, including the burden of domestic chores, play a role in constraining their ability to work. All this leads to substantial gender gaps in earnings and productivity, which in turn reduces women's bargaining power and voice as well as their ability to negotiate their productive work. This section analyzes three issues related to women's (a) productivity in agriculture, (b) productivity in formal employment, and (c) entrepreneurship.

Female-managed plots of land are 62 percent less productive than those managed by men. Most of the gender gap is due to differences in endowments (for example, access to productive land, inputs, extension services, agricultural equipment, credit, and level of education and literacy), meaning that if men and women had access to the same resources, the gender gap in agricultural productivity would be reduced. The fact that women generally farm smaller plots is associated with the gender gap in productivity. Women's lower access to farm labor and typical crop choices are also correlated with this gender gap, as it narrows the more women cultivate millet, sorghum, and rice.

Women are 9 percent less likely to be in formal employment than are men; however, there is no gender gap in wages for those formally employed. Women in formal employment are much more likely to be literate and to have a secondary or tertiary education than women in informal employment. They are also more likely to be single, widowed, or separated. Moreover, women's lower propensity to be in formal employment is linked to women having lower levels of education. Married women in either monogamous or polygamous unions are also less likely to have formal employment. Nevertheless, women in formal employment have similar wages, on average, to their male counterparts within the same sectors and with similar education levels. There is occupational segregation by gender to the extent that men are more likely to work in construction, transportation, communication, agriculture, and livestock breeding, while women are more likely to work in education, health care, hospitality, and personal services.

Despite accounting for 57 percent of enterprises, female-owned firms make 77 percent less profit than male-owned firms. Female entrepreneurs are also much less likely to have access to electricity, running water, machinery, bank accounts, or telephones than male entrepreneurs. Part of the gender gap in enterprise profits is due to sectoral segregation. More women entrepreneurs in sales and repairs of motor vehicles would be associated with a smaller gender gap in profit. However, most of the gender gap in profits comes from differences in returns to factors of production, revealing underlying biases.

Weak public administration

Service delivery is limited, costly, and constrained by the country's large size and sparse population density.[9] Low government capacity and high concentration of administration in the capital, N'Djamena, translates into a low allocation of public resources for implementing pro-poor policies in rural areas. Moreover, fiscal transfers are limited by low non-oil revenue mobilization, averaging 8.1 percent of GDP in 2018—significantly lower than the CEMAC and Sahel averages of 12.8 percent and 15 percent of GDP, respectively. Finally, while transparency and accountability are improving, substantial efforts are needed to address citizen grievances, which are exacerbated by limited forums for the public to be heard and access information.

Chad's service delivery performance is worse than the average of regional comparators. Its performance is lower than the average of G5 Sahel, SSA, Middle East and North Africa, and conflict-affected countries (for example, Afghanistan and Iraq) on access to electricity (11.8 percent), access to basic drinking water (38.7 percent), literacy (22.3 percent), and life expectancy (53.7 years) (table 2.1). The poor quality of the country's service delivery particularly affects youth, women, marginalized populations, and rural households. This is accentuated by the country's large size and a sparse geographic population density of 12 persons/km² (compared to the SSA average of 49 persons/km²), which increases the cost to expand essential services. While 68.85 percent of the urban

TABLE 2.1 **Key service delivery indicators**

YEAR(S)		CHAD	G5 SAHEL	SSA	MNA	AFGHANISTAN	IRAQ
2010–18	Average GDP per capita growth (annual %)	0.14	1.4	0.9	1.3	1.8	2.4
2018	Lower-middle-income poverty rate (US$3.20/day)	68.1	63.2	..	19.8	..	..
2017	Life expectancy at birth, total (years)	53.7	59.8	61.3	74.1	64.5	70.4
2018	Rural population (% of total population)	77.0	67.0	59.8	34.6	74.5	29.5
2018	Access to electricity (% of population)	11.8	27.8	47.7	96.5	97.7	99.9
2017	Individuals using the internet (% pop.)	6.5	13.3	25.4	65.1	13.5	75.0
2017	Access to basic drinking water (% pop.)	38.7	57.2	60.9	94.1	67.1	96.5
2012–18	Literacy rate, adult total (% ages ≥15)	22.3	36.6	65.6	79.0	43.0	85.6
2016–18	Fertility rate, total (births per woman)	5.7	5.7	4.7	2.8	4.6	3.7
2017–18	Youth unemployment (% ages 15–24)	3.0	8.3	11.5	27.5	17.3	25.3
2018	Employment in agriculture (% of total)	76.7	58.6	53.0	16.0	43.4	18.4
2017	UN Human Development Index (HDI) score	0.4	0.4	0.5	0.8	0.5	0.7
2018	WGI Government Effectiveness score	−1.5	−0.9	−0.8	−0.3	−1.5	−1.3

Sources: World Development Indicators, (https://data.worldbank.org/indicator) and World Bank 2020b.
Note: .. = negligible; G5 Sahel = Burkina Faso, Chad, Mali, Mauritania, and Niger; MNA = Middle East and North Africa region; SSA = Sub-Saharan Africa; WGI = Worldwide Governance Indicators.

population has access to basic drinking water, it falls to 29.47 percent in rural areas.[10] The situation is similar for electricity, with 41.84 percent of the urban population having access to electricity, compared to only 2.75 percent of the rural population.[11]

Government effectiveness is constrained by limited public administration capacity, a concentration of resources and decision-making in the capital city, low levels of revenues, and sensitivity to shocks such as COVID-19. Chad's institutional capacity is fragile (with a 2009–19 Country Policy and Institutional Assessment [CPIA] average of 2.6) and highly concentrated, with 55 percent of civil servants based in N'Djamena and almost 100 percent of financial resources executed at the central ministry level (World Bank 2021b). The decentralization initiated in 2012 is still largely in the planning stages. Transfer of resources and responsibilities has been limited, and the scale-up of transfers is hampered by insufficient local capacity and inadequate central resource management institutions to formulate, plan, and execute public policies as well as to manage crises. Consequently, there are insufficient linkages between policy planning, implementation, and citizens' service delivery needs. The absence of holistic crisis response plans, along with inadequate institutional frameworks and procedures, has also limited the efficiency of the government's response to crises, eroding the social contract and trust in the state.

Chad's performance on selected indicators of transparency, accountability, and corruption is below that of peers in the Sahel region and SSA. In 2019, Chad scored 20 on Transparency International's Corruption Perceptions Index, ranking 162nd out of 180 countries—below all G5 Sahel and CEMAC peer countries (table 2.2), with the exception of the Republic of Congo (19) and Equatorial Guinea (16). While Chad's Open Budget Index score improved significantly, from 0 in 2010 to 14 in 2019, it remained below the average of G5 Sahel (22.5), CEMAC (15.6), and SSA (31). Chad's performance on the CPIA in terms of transparency, accountability, and corruption was an average of 2.5 in 2018—comparable to that of CEMAC peers, but below the average for G5 Sahel (3.0).

TABLE 2.2 **Transparency Indexes, Chad and selected groups**

INDEX	CHAD	G5 SAHEL	CEMAC	SSA	MNA
Transparency International Corruption Perception Index, 2019	20	29.8	22.7	32.3	38.5
Open Budget Index Score, 2019	14	22.5	15.6	31.0	21.8
CPIA transparency, accountability, corruption (IDA countries), 2018	2.5	3.0	2.4	2.7	2.0

Sources: Transparency International and World Bank staff estimates.
Note: CEMAC = Economic and Monetary Community of Central Africa; CPIA = Country Policy and Institutional Assessment; G5 Sahel = Burkina Faso, Chad, Mali, Mauritania, and Niger; IDA = International Development Association (of the World Bank Group); MNA = Middle East and North Africa; SSA = Sub-Saharan Africa.

The deteriorating security situation in Chad and the Sahel has led to an increase in the share of government expenditures allocated to national defense.[12] Chad plays an important role in the regional fight against extremist groups. This has, however, reduced the already-limited level of public resources available for other sectors, including pro-poor social sectors such as education and health (World Bank 2019a). Moreover, the inflow of refugees from neighboring countries has increased the pressure on already-stretched public service providers (World Bank 2019b).

GROWING CONSTRAINTS NOT COVERED BY THE 2015 SCD

Violence and political fragility

While Chad has enjoyed relative stability after decades of major armed conflicts, it remains vulnerable to localized conflicts and violence.[13] Since 2016, violent conflicts in neighboring countries—such as Libya in the north, the Central African Republic in the south, and Nigeria in the southwest—pose a significant security threat to Chad. This threat materialized in April 2021 in a rebellion that originated at the Libyan border and led to the death of President Idriss Déby, who had been reelected for a sixth term on April 19, 2021. This led to the ongoing military-led political transition.

The number and types of localized conflicts and violent events in Chad have risen significantly since 2015 (map 2.1). While conflict and violent events predominated in the Lake Chad region in 2015, they affected almost all regions of the country by 2018. The rise of the terrorist group Boko Haram in 2015 led to nearly two-thirds of all armed, organized political violence taking place in the Lake Chad region, and nearly one-third of all violence in Chad occurred there in 2019. This trend continued in the first quarter of 2020 due to the rise in Boko Haram attacks and violence in the Lake Chad region. In 2018, violence in the Tibesti region spiked, with 40 percent of all the violence in Chad taking place there that year. The occurrence of violence in the region has since declined, and it represented less than 10 percent of all violence in the country in 2019. However, there was a steep rise in violence in both Ouaddaï and Sila provinces in 2019, and these provinces were home to nearly one-quarter of all violence in Chad that year, due to the rise in intercommunal violence. Finally, there has been a significant rise in political unrest in the N'Djamena region, leading to an increase in violence involving civilian and security forces, which accounted for 13 percent of all violent events in the country in 2019. There has also been a steep rise in armed conflict, largely driven by both clashes between Boko Haram and state forces and

MAP 2.1

Political violence in Chad, by event type, 2013–20

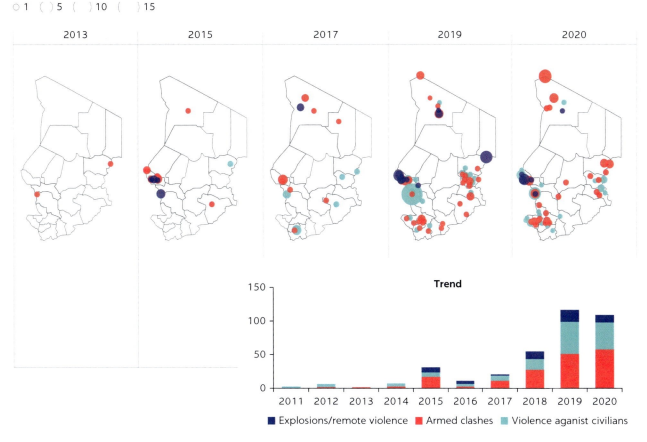

Source: World Bank, adapted from Armed Conflict Location and Event Data Project (database), Madison, WI (accessed June 17, 2020), https://acleddata.com/dashboard/#/dashboard.

clashes between state forces, ethnic militias, and other intercommunal groups, as well as violence against civilians and between state forces and Boko Haram.

Boko Haram and communal militias have been the main groups responsible for the rise in violent events. The most dramatic increase has been the rise in activities involving communal militias, which include ethnic militias, pastoralists, farmers, and other groups. In addition, the rise in attacks by Boko Haram has led to a rise in activities involving rebel groups and the state forces that they combat.

Regional and localized conflicts have diverted public resources away from human development and productive sectors, disrupted value chains, and lowered productivity. The fiscal costs of insecurity have effectively crowded out investment expenditures in growth-enhancing sectors such as health and education. In 2019, Chad spent 14 percent of total government spending on the military, the highest among in G5 Sahel countries,[14] while it dedicated 6 percent and 11 percent to health and education, respectively. The Boko Haram conflict in the Lake Chad region has disrupted trade between Chad and its neighbors Cameroon and Nigeria, specifically the livestock trade, which is a major source of Chadian exports. The conflict has also disrupted agriculture and fisheries in the region, which has one of the most productive agriculture basins. Other localized conflicts continue to increase the risk for investment and business development, as entrepreneurs are uncertain about the returns on their work and investments.

Fall in oil revenue and challenges to macroeconomic management

Falling and volatile oil revenue has been a major determinant of Chad's growth dynamic. Since the 2014–15 price shock, oil prices have remained low, reducing the size of the oil sector. Oil accounted for only about 15 percent of GDP in 2015–20, down from 25 percent in 2005–14. However, oil revenue still accounted for about 38 percent of total public revenue between 2015 and 2020, underscoring the importance of economic diversification for public financial stability.[15]

The country has implemented a painful fiscal consolidation program to improve debt sustainability. Following the 2014–15 oil price shock, the decline in oil revenues (figure 2.6) and public spending prompted the government to implement a fiscal consolidation program. The authorities contained the wage bill and strengthened non-oil revenue mobilization efforts. Consequently, the overall fiscal deficit improved from 5.8 percent of non-oil GDP in 2015 to 0.8 percent in 2019 (figure 2.7). The government also successfully restructured its debt with Glencore, its main private creditor, which restored liquidity and debt sustainability in 2018. While total public debt fell from a peak of 54.8 percent of GDP in 2016 to 44.3 percent in 2019, Chad remains at high risk of debt distress.

The absence of a clear strategy for managing oil price volatility has hampered Chad's capacity to take full advantage of its oil resources (World Bank 2018). At the beginning of the Chad-Cameroon pipeline project, the government adopted an oil revenue management mechanism that included a stabilization account. However, a new revenue management law was promulgated without any stabilization or saving function. It allowed oil revenues to be used to strengthen Chad's military and resulted in greater elite capture (World Bank 2019b). As a result, the oil price shock of 2014–15 forced the government to pursue severe fiscal adjustment and subsequently fiscal consolidation. In November 2019, with World Bank support, the government adopted a new oil revenue management framework to support countercyclical expenditure policies in the face of oil price and production volatility. Through the adoption of the new oil

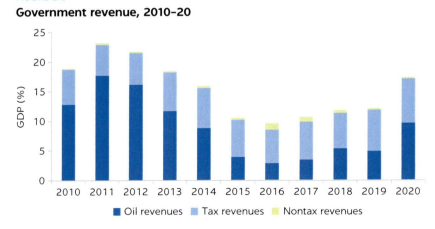

FIGURE 2.6
Government revenue, 2010–20

Sources: Bank of Central African States (BEAC) and Chad authorities.

FIGURE 2.7
Fiscal and current account balances, 2010–20

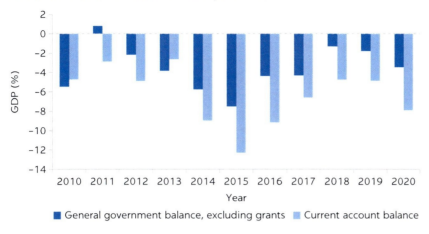

Sources: Bank of Central African States (BEAC) and Chad authorities.

revenue management mechanism, the government has embraced the concept of setting aside oil revenue to smooth unexpected future revenue shortfalls (Campagne, Kitzmuller, and Tordo 2020).

COVID-19 and its related shocks are showing once more that an overreliance on oil revenue is detrimental to Chad's fiscal sustainability and economy. Lower-than-expected production in 2020, combined with the sharp decrease in oil prices and the potential contraction of the economy due to the pandemic, led to an increase in the public debt-to-GDP ratio beyond the 41.2 percent projected for 2020. In nominal terms, total exports decreased by 20.4 percent in 2020 due to the impact of COVID-19 on global demand, the oil price shock, and border closures. As a result, Chad's savings/investment balance deteriorated, and the current account deficit widened to 9.7 percent.

Moreover, the Dutch disease (that is, labor reallocation from low-productivity non-oil sectors to highly productive activities) that plagues resource-rich countries is an obstacle to structural change. Over the past decade, oil has accounted for more than 84 percent of Chad's total exports, and it reached 92 percent in 2018. The sectoral composition of the economy has remained broadly unchanged, with a low share of manufacturing oscillating around a low 8 percent of GDP—centered on state-owned enterprises (SOEs) and an atypical declining share of the services sector. More than 80 percent of Chad's population rely on agriculture for their livelihoods and work as subsistence farmers in low-productivity informal activities, as Chad's domestic market is too small and uncompetitive to foster agricultural productivity.

Assessments of the 2019 current account and real effective exchange rate (REER) suggest an overvaluation and a weaker external position than implied by fundamentals and desirable policies for the CEMAC region (IMF 2019). The REER depreciated by about 6 percent throughout 2019, mainly reflecting a weakening of the euro versus the US dollar. The IMF suggests an overvaluation of 11.4 percent, with the 2019 current account deficit estimated at 2.5 percent of GDP, against a norm of 0.3 percent GDP surplus (assuming an elasticity of the current account to REER of −0.25). The external position at the end of 2019 was assessed to be weaker than expected, despite a positive contribution from the adjustment in the fiscal balance, health expenditures, and reserves.

Environment and climate change

Chad is the world's most vulnerable country in terms of climate change, and the least ready to deal with climate change impacts, according to the Notre Dame Global Adaptation Initiative (ND-GAIN) Country Index.[16] The impact of climate change on the large natural, agro-sylvo-pastoral, fishery, and human hydrographic systems in the Lake Chad basin is significant and has been increasing. Between 2015 and 2021, climate change exacerbated desertification, forest degradation, the degradation of the productive potential of soil, competition for access to resources, the degradation of natural habitats, the loss of biodiversity, the depletion of water tables, and the silting of oases.[17] Effects include changes to the agricultural seasons, disturbances in the biological cycles of crops, a reduction in cereal crop production, an extension of the time and space necessary for transhumance, the degradation of protected areas and wetlands, and an increase in bush fires. Hence, water is the main vector through which climate change manifests in a setting such as Chad, with potentially spiraling effects if tipping points (particularly around groundwater-dependent ecosystems around Lake Chad) are reached.

Since the country's economy is based on natural resources, the impact of climate change is a particularly serious challenge for Chad.[18] The environment is neither a sector of economic activity, like agriculture or industry, nor a form of infrastructure, like urban sewer systems or roads. Instead, it is an input for almost every productive activity in the country. Most production systems have an impact on the environment, which threatens their own sustainability. The impact of climate-related disasters such as droughts or floods becomes magnified in Chad because of the lack of resources to manage or prevent them.

Poaching is another example of unsustainable management of natural resources. For example, Chad's elephant population fell from an estimated 300,000 in the 1930s to 450 animals in 2010, before it started to increase again for the first time in decades (Antonínová, Malachie, and Banymary 2014).

Climate predictions for Chad hint at increased volatility in rainfall and more extreme weather events in the coming years, which—in combination with urbanization dynamics—may lead to more frequent and significant urban flooding. In the Sahel region, there is seasonal, interannual, and interdecadal variability in annual rainfall and extreme weather events, resulting in significant flash floods and riverine overflowing, heavily affecting urban areas. Climate change is exacerbating more frequent, intense, and longer droughts and more extreme rainfall and flooding. N'Djamena has a particular history of high-impact floods due to its low declivity and interannual volatility in peak flows of the Chari and Logone rivers and urbanization trends.

Urban pollution is another important growing dimension of the environmental challenges faced in Chad. Increasing waste, low collection rates, and lack of sanitary landfills, sorting equipment, and recycling facilities increase pollution. The situation is alarming in urban areas, where the highest volumes of waste are concentrated. For example, the city of N'Djamena generates about 600 tons of solid waste per day, of which less than 20 percent is collected and transferred to landfills. In some districts of the city, as little as 5 percent of solid waste is collected, with the rest being dumped on roads, markets, and other public sites (Bantin and Jun 2018; Warri 2012).

NOTES

1. This constraint was included in the "access to physical and human capital" constraint in the 2015 SCD, and it has been exacerbated by lack of financing since 2015.
2. Safe or improved drinking water refers to "basic water," as defined in the SDGs as drinking water from an improved water source located on premises (piped water) or a source (for example, tube wells, boreholes, protected dug wells, protected springs, and rainwater collection) that can be reached with no more than a 30-minute round trip.
3. This constraint was included in the "social returns to economic activities in the rural sector" constraint.
4. Land ownership refers mainly to usage, which means that even if they do not have the documentation, they are able to use the land as a productive asset.
5. This constraint was included in the "access to physical and human capital" constraint in the 2015 SCD, and it has been exacerbated by lack of financing since 2015 and by the COVID-19 crisis.
6. Apart from weak expenditures, there are delays in budget preparation, and public procurement remains cumbersome.
7. This constraint was included in the "access to physical and human capital" constraint in the 2015 SCD.
8. The labor force participation rate is defined as the proportion of the working-age population (ages 15–64 years) that is either working or actively looking for work. Unpaid and domestic care work is not included in this definition due to a lack of available data.
9. This constraint was included in the "individual appropriation of returns to investment and entrepreneurship" and "authorities' incentives and capacity to address constraints to poverty reduction" constraints in the 2015 SCD.
10. World Development Indicators (WDI): People using at least basic drinking water services (percent of population) indicator.
11. WDI: Access to electricity (percent of population) indicator.
12. WDI: Military expenditures (percent of general government expenditures) indicator.
13. In this section, fragility refers to security and political fragility.
14. During the last civil war between 2005 and 2009, military expenditures increased by about 26 percentage points, while health and education expenditures decreased by 8.4 and 5.2 percentage points, respectively.
15. The country has been able to adjust thanks to reforms and the support of donors.
16. Notre Dame Global Adaptation Initiative (ND-GAIN) Country Index, https://gain.nd.edu/our-work/country-index/.
17. Natural resource degradation in Chad may be attributed to population growth, climate change, recurrent warfare, and social and cultural patterns. These factors lead to changes in agriculture, forestry, livestock production, and fisheries.
18. Approximately 80 percent of the population is active in the agriculture and livestock sectors.

REFERENCES

Antonínová, M., D. N. Malachie, and D. Banymary. 2014. "National Elephant Conservation and Management Strategy for Chad (NECMSC) 2015–2019." Working document, Chad.

Bantin, A. B., and X. Jun. 2018. "Environmental Impact of Household Garbage on Population and Groundwater: Case of the City of N'Djamena, Chad." *Research & Reviews: Journal of Ecology and Environmental Sciences*, e-ISSN: 2347-7830.

Campagne, Benoît, Markus Kitzmuller, and Silvana Tordo. 2020. "Designing Oil Revenue Management Mechanisms: An Application to Chad." Policy Research Working Paper 9402, World Bank, Washington, DC. https://openknowledge.worldbank.org/handle/10986/34500.

Chad INSEED (Tchad, Institut National de la Statistique, des Études Économiques et Démographiques). 2018. *Tchad, Quatrieme enquête sur la consommation et le secteur informel au Tchad-ECOSIT 4*.

Chad Santé (Ministère de la Santé Publique). 2018. "Plan national de développement sanitaire (PNDS3: 2017–2021)." January. République du Tchad, Ministère de la Santé Publique, N'Djamena.

IMF (International Monetary Fund). 2019. "Central African Economic and Monetary Community—Common Policies in Support of Member Countries Reform Programs." IMF Country Report 19/383, World Bank Group, Washington, DC. https://www.imf.org/en/Publications/CR/Issues/2019/12/20/Central-African-Economic-and-Monetary-Community-CEMAC-Staff-Report-on-the-Common-Policies-in-48903.

UNESCO (United Nations Educational, Scientific, and Cultural Organization). 2016. "Rapport d'état du système éducatif national du Tchad: Éléments d'analyse pour une refondation de l'école, République du Tchad." UNESCO, UNICEF, IIPE Pôle de Dakar. https://unesdoc.unesco.org/ark:/48223/pf0000247447.

Warri, S. 2012. "Problématique de la gestion des déchets ménagers urbains de la ville de N'Djamena: Cas du 8eme arrondissement." Thèse de master, Institut International d'Ingénierie de l'Eau et de l'Environnement.

World Bank. 2018. "Escaping Chad's Growth Labyrinth: Disentangling Constraints from Opportunities and Finding a Path to Sustainable Growth." World Bank. https://elibrary.worldbank.org/doi/pdf/10.1596/30941.

World Bank. 2019a. "Chad Public Expenditure Analysis: Fiscal Space for Productive Social Sectors Expenditure." World Bank, Washington, DC. https://openknowledge.worldbank.org/handle/10986/34616.

World Bank. 2019b. *Rapport Evaluation des Risques et de la Résilience dans la région du Sahel*. Unpublished paper.

World Bank. 2020a. "Chad: Human Capital Index 2020." https://databank.worldbank.org/data/download/hci/HCI_2pager_TCD.pdf.

World Bank. 2020b. "Macro Poverty Outlook: Country-by-Country Analysis and Projections for the Developing World." World Bank, Washington, DC. https://thedocs.worldbank.org/en/doc/77351105a334213c64122e44c2efe523-0500072021/related/mpo-sm20.pdf.

World Bank. 2021a. "Chad: The Economic Benefits of a Post-COVID-19 Gender-Equitable Society." World Bank, Washington, DC. https://openknowledge.worldbank.org/handle/10986/36444.

World Bank, 2021b. "Chad Risk and Resilience Assessment." Unpublished paper.

3 Key Prerequisites to Seize Opportunities

OVERVIEW

Chad will be unable to fully pursue the identified pathways unless it more effectively addresses the drivers underlying the increase in fragility, conflict, and violence in the country. Making institutions more accountable and inclusive remains a key policy priority, and this could be achieved by both (a) reducing regional imbalances and exclusion by investing in more and better services in peripheral and underserved areas that are the most affected by conflict or at risk of conflict and (b) strengthening governance and accountability to enhance the social contract and improve public trust. Promoting a green economy and improving the management of natural resources will be key to addressing climate change and supporting economic inclusion. The successful pursuit of the pathways is also dependent on adequate macrofiscal management and a business-friendly environment, including adequate oil revenue management, non-oil revenue mobilization, sustainable public financial management (PFM), and regional integration.

ADDRESSING CONSTRAINTS

This Systematic Country Diagnostic identifies three cross-cutting prerequisites and three pathways to address the binding constraints on poverty reduction described in chapter 2. Several criteria are used to identify these most critical prerequisites and pathways. The first three criteria are related to the impact on the goals: improving livelihoods, creating jobs, and strengthening the social contract. To catalyze private investment and job creation, the following three prerequisites are identified: (a) strengthening the social contract through accountable and inclusive institutions, (b) improving the management of natural resources and adapting to climate change, and (c) achieving adequate macrofiscal management as well as a business-friendly environment; these are cross-cutting solutions to address some identified constraints. To raise worker productivity and improve access to improved earning opportunities, the following three pathways are emphasized: (a) supporting improvements in human capital to improve worker productivity, (b) improving infrastructure to raise productivity, and

(c) promoting sectors with a strategic advantage for more and better jobs. The remaining two criteria are political and economic feasibility (which involves assessing Chad's political economy and the governance and institutional challenges that would impact the ability to address the identified constraint) and the time horizon impact (which involves an assessment of the time frame under which the impact can be expected to be realized over the short and long terms).[1]

STRENGTHENING THE SOCIAL CONTRACT THROUGH ACCOUNTABLE AND INCLUSIVE INSTITUTIONS

The emergence of violent conflicts in the Sahel has been associated with increased social exclusion, inequality, and marginalization. The countries in the area and their development partners have traditionally underinvested in many of the regions located in border and peripheral areas, due to limited resources and a focus on the agriculture sector in more densely populated areas (World Bank 2019a). Developments in the Sahel call for renewed efforts to link security and development policies, and countries' structural redeployment efforts need to focus on historically underserved areas outside the capital cities. In Chad, the deployment of state forces must be accompanied by broader efforts to improve the relationship between the state and citizens, as public policies that only focus on certain regions or sectors undermine the legitimacy of the state (World Bank 2018b). While the government is taking a range of actions to ensure an inclusive political transition, provide security to the population, and increase access to services in at-risk and conflict affected areas, including justice services, as part of Chad's action plan under the Prevention and Resilience Allocation, more needs to be done to address regional imbalances and strengthen the social contract.

Reducing regional imbalances and exclusion that fuel resentment and growing grievances

To reduce regional imbalances and social exclusion, the authorities should consider the following:

- *Strengthening inclusive and transparent governance.* To achieve a more inclusive development model and sustainable peace, the government needs to prioritize the creation of inclusive, transparent, and accountable institutions. The combination of overcentralized governance with poor government effectiveness and lack of accountability fosters informal payments and social exclusion. This has been recognized by the government of Chad in the National Development Plan 2017–2021 and during the preparation of the Prevention and Resilience Allocation Eligibility Note. The government should, therefore, prioritize the fight against corruption and impunity; support and strengthen civil society; improve public sector administration by establishing a transparent and efficient budgeting process; improve the transparency of state-owned enterprises (SOEs), particularly in the oil sector; and advance the decentralization process to strengthen local governance.
- *Strengthening inclusion and subnational governance as well as investing in human capital across the country.* The bulk of public spending and service

delivery occurs in N'Djamena, to the detriment of peripheral regions, which can fuel social exclusion at the territorial level. Likewise, women and youth are marginalized at the social, economic, and political levels. To reduce social exclusion and regional imbalances that are the root causes of Chad's conflicts, the government should focus on strengthening local governance and service delivery and accelerating human capital development in conflict-affected, at-risk, and peripheral areas. Applying a spatial approach to analyzing regional imbalances and exclusion and designing policies and territorial development strategies by focusing on poverty-stricken and fragility, conflict, and violence (FCV)–affected areas could address structural underinvestment in certain regions and populations. The government should also empower local authorities in the management of critical socioeconomic areas to reduce spatial inequalities.

- *Strengthening security, the rule of law, justice, and dispute resolution mechanisms.* Populations in conflict-affected areas suffer insecurity and lack of redress while existing conflict resolution mechanisms are unable to mediate conflicts around natural resources in various parts of the country. The security sector suffers from politization, and security forces are at times also a source of tension with the public. The justice sector's lack of independence from the executive branch and limited financial resources prevent it from effectively implementing justice and mitigating conflicts. As a result, traditional justice has remained an alternative to formal judicial services over the years. Traditional justice, however, has its limitations, including the exclusion of women and youth due to cultural discrimination and a growing inability to resolve intercommunal conflicts, particularly between farmers and pastoralists. Therefore, reestablishing security and the rule of law at the subnational level by strengthening the technical and organizational capacity of the local police, gendarmes, and Garde Nationale et Nomade du Tchad is a priority. Other priorities include (a) developing a functional and harmonized justice system by reinforcing the capacity of judiciary staff; (b) increasing the number of tribunals, especially in underprivileged and FCV-affected areas; (c) increasing the number of legal clinics and informing the public of their legal rights; and (d) providing sufficient support and funding to traditional mechanisms of conflict resolution that can complement the formal justice system.

- *Strengthening natural resource governance and intercommunal reconciliation.* Inter- and intracommunal conflicts over access to resources, particularly water and land, have been increasing and occur in almost every region of the country. They are exacerbated by climatic variations and amplified by the weak governance of land, outdated pastoralism laws, and the growing inefficiency of traditional conflict resolution mechanisms. Therefore, natural resource governance should be strengthened by improving land governance measures (including land titling and tenure) and pastoral-transhumance regulations for moving herds (including updating pastoral laws and the delineation of transhumance corridors). Furthermore, measures are needed to support marginalized pastoral populations, such as adequate mobile delivery of health and education services adapted to these populations' needs. Water points around pastoral transhumance corridors must be added and properly managed in collaboration and negotiation between pastoralists and host communities.

Improving service delivery to enhance the social contract and public trust

To improve service delivery, the authorities should consider the following:

- *Building core institutions and allocating an appropriate level of resources to local governments for service delivery.* Service delivery is limited in Chad, particularly for youth, women, marginalized populations, and residents in rural areas. This is exacerbated by the country's large size and a sparse population density of 12 persons/km² (compared to the SSA average of 49 persons/km²), which increases the cost to expand essential services such as health, education, water, and sanitation. The transfer of resources and responsibilities from central to local government authorities remains limited. Moreover, the scale-up of transfers is hampered by insufficient local capacity and inadequate central public financial management (PFM) and human resources management (HRM) systems as well as institutions to formulate, plan, and execute public policies and manage crises such as the COVID-19 pandemic.
- *Extending capacity building to provinces, departments, and municipalities to pave the way for a transfer of PFM competency from central to local government authorities.* Because of their proximity to citizens, local governments are in a better position to provide high-quality services to their constituencies. They must, however, have the financial and human resources as well as the technical capacities and skills to provide these services. The Chadian authorities in the 2017–2021 National Development Plan recognize that insufficient resources and skills hamper the ability of municipalities to provide services. It is therefore important to strengthen their capacity to formulate citizens' needs and spending priorities, implement programs, and report on the use of funds and results to improve service delivery.
- *Implementing national and sectoral HRM strategies that promote the deployment of competent technical staff in local communities while enabling communities to recruit and train local staff with extensive field experience.* This will require reviewing current financial and nonfinancial incentive programs as well as career advancement opportunities to ensure that they promote the deployment of public servants in difficult geographic areas where technical skills are scarce. Citizen monitoring, combined with public administration oversight, should be implemented to ensure that only eligible deployed personnel receive deployment incentives. In addition, the recruitment of local staff and extensive training will create high-quality jobs in local communities while providing services tailored to local needs.
- *Strengthening central systems for transferring financial resources from central to local government authorities.* First, the legal framework that defines service functions and responsibilities of each level of government needs to be updated for coherence and comprehensiveness. Second, a multiyear perspective for budget planning should be implemented at central and local levels to ensure predictability of transfers to subnational governments. Third, streamlining the expenditure chain and setting up an efficient computerized system will improve the timeliness of transfers and local government budget execution rates. Finally, building capacity of internal and external audit institutions (supreme audit institutions, general inspection of finance, and so on) will improve accountability and transparency at national and subnational levels.

- *Fostering a strong and effective civil society to strengthen governance and accountability.* In addition to participatory planning, budgeting, and monitoring, the ability of citizens to elect their local representatives is crucial for improving citizen participation and public accountability in service delivery. The government should commit to timely and transparent local elections, encourage the plurality of Chad's civil society, and work with civil society organizations to set up efficient communication channels between citizens and government authorities. In accordance with the Chadian Constitution, local representatives must be elected by universal suffrage every six years. However, the last local elections were held in January 2012.

ADAPTING TO CLIMATE CHANGE AND IMPROVING THE MANAGEMENT OF NATURAL RESOURCES

Addressing climate change by promoting a green economy

A successful strategy to green the economy involves environmental and social full-cost pricing of energy and material inputs to discourage unsustainable production and consumption. In general, such a strategy is diametrically opposite to one where companies compete on price, not quality; externalize social and environmental costs; and seek out the cheapest inputs of materials and labor. Natural capital assets must be included on a country's balance sheet.

To promote a green economy, the authorities should consider the following:

- *Designing and implementing key policies for green jobs.* First, the government needs to address its natural capital assets through landscape and watershed management, ecosystem restoration, sustainable management of forests, and regenerative agriculture and food systems that can create jobs quickly. These activities generate long-term benefits thanks to reduced water scarcity or flood damages, lower carbon emissions, and higher agricultural productivity and food security. They can also protect biodiversity and maintain or enhance ecosystem services that can reduce investment needs. Second, it needs to adopt innovative policies to overcome barriers and create incentives to renewable energy development, including by adopting feed-in laws that secure access to the electrical grid at guaranteed prices. Third, the country should adopt ecolabels for all consumer products to ensure that consumers have access to information needed for responsible purchasing decisions, which in turn would encourage manufacturers to design and market more ecofriendly products. Finally, the authorities need to ensure that regulatory tools are used to develop greener technologies, products, and services—and thus green employment. These tools include land-use policies, building codes, energy-efficiency standards (for appliances, vehicles, and so on), and targets for renewable energy production.
- *Reforming fiscal policy to promote green energy.* This includes (a) scaling up and replicating ecotaxes, as ecotax revenues can be used to lighten the tax burden on labor while discouraging polluting and carbon-intensive economic activities; (b) reducing support for fossil fuels and providing greater funding for renewable energy and efficient technologies; and (c) phasing out subsidies for environmentally harmful industries (such as electricity supply, slaughter slabs, and so on) and shifting a portion or all of those funds to renewable energy, efficient technologies, clean production methods, and public transit.

- *Strengthening policies and regulation in priority infrastructure sectors such as energy, water, sanitation (including waste management), and transport to promote the use of green technologies and climate-resilient design as well as the development of green businesses.* Clean energy infrastructure is labor-intensive in the early stages, which is important to consider while planning for economic diversification away from oil production. The authorities can promote job creation through nature-based solutions and natural resource management by, for example, investing in forests, watersheds, and land restoration. Indeed, nature-based solutions and hybrid systems that combine infrastructure with ecosystem services are labor intensive, have low overall costs, and result in benefits such as higher agricultural productivity and reduced drought and flood losses. Moreover, the government needs to adopt policies aimed at opening markets and crowding in private investment.

- *Adopting short-term reforms to reduce the environmental footprint of the oil and gas sector, including the regulation of gas flaring and methane emissions, waste management, and produced water management.* However, Chad should also explore a strategy to transition out of fossil fuels to avoid having stranded assets. There are opportunities to leverage the oil and gas sector, such as (a) exploiting advanced data management (for example, identifying a new business segment to integrate sustainable development variables in the oil and gas sector); (b) repurposing water used in the oil production process; and (c) using existing petroleum infrastructure for other strategic industries (World Bank 2020). The government should work with oil and water companies as well with local communities to identify ways to use produced water (which is a by-product of oil and gas production) for irrigation to increase agricultural productivity. Leveraging oil sector–related investments through shared use could help narrow the gap in public infrastructure funding. Moreover, Chad could exploit natural gas and renewable energy to promote low-carbon electricity generation, as part of its strategic objective to increase access to electricity and promote climate-smart growth.

Achieving an efficient natural resource management

A significant oil dividend was not properly leveraged to foster structural long-term growth (World Bank 2018a). Chad appears to have missed a great opportunity to boost and sustain GDP per capita levels and translate oil revenues into permanently faster GDP growth through investment in human capital and infrastructure. Oil has made the country's economy less competitive and more vulnerable to exogenous shocks. Notably, export diversification was already low before the discovery of oil, but declined even further after 2003, exposing Chad's economy to international oil price cycles and shocks. Meanwhile, large capital inflows triggered by oil production and exports may have reduced external competitiveness in other sectors due to Dutch disease dynamics, resulting in the shift of sector shares of GDP toward nontradable and relatively unproductive (low skill) services. Given that Chad's monetary and exchange rate policies are managed by the regional Bank of Central African States (BEAC), regional monetary authorities should support economic transformation with a monetary policy that avoids exchange rate overvaluation and favors credit to the private sector and private sector competitiveness.

To improve the management of oil and natural resource revenues, the authorities should consider the following:

- *Creating a fiscal framework conducive to the efficient management of oil-based revenues.* The management of oil-based revenues is complex and presents numerous challenges involving the nonrenewable nature of extractive resources and the volatility of oil prices. To ensure the efficient management of natural resource revenue, the government should create a fiscal framework consisting of (a) budget tracking indicators, (b) fiscal rules that ensure sound management of volatile revenue based on short-term oil prices, (c) fiscal sustainability criteria, and (d) rules for the accumulation and management of monetary reserves.
- *Ensuring the management of oil revenues can smooth economic cycles and create buffers ready to absorb commodity price shocks.* During economic upturns, the government should maintain fiscal balances in a stabilization fund to ensure the availability of sufficient financial resources in the event of a negative oil price shock. It could also design and implement a trajectory for the accumulation of reserves to build a stabilization buffer and avoid an abrupt adjustment in government spending. Finally, it could establish clear rules for drawdowns of the stabilization fund and strictly eliminate ad hoc payments and withdrawals. To reduce revenue volatility, the government established a petroleum revenue management mechanism, with support from the World Bank, in November 2019, to help shore up the effects of unexpected revenue shortfalls (World Bank 2019c). While the stabilization account has received its first fourth deposits, accounting for CFAF 10 billion, this is insufficient to act as an effective buffer in the current context. It is therefore critical for the government to create more fiscal room to reduce its dependence on current oil revenue.
- *Creating well-designed fiscal institutions responsible for developing and maintaining sound fiscal policies while guaranteeing transparency within independent forecasting bodies.* Chad's PFM system should be sufficiently robust to (a) provide reasonable forecasts for oil prices, production, and fiscal revenues as well as analyze related risks; (b) carry out medium-term budget planning; (c) facilitate investment project appraisal, selection, and implementation to ensure that resource revenues are used to support long-term economic development; (d) integrate cash management and minimize financing costs to ensure a single account exists between the budget and any natural resource fund; and (e) ensure transparency in the collection and utilization of natural resource revenues and other available resources through appropriate fiscal accounting, reporting, and auditing. When creating fiscal institutions, the government should consider giving prominence to fiscal transparency and good governance. Finally, the country should ensure a good return on infrastructure investments funded with oil revenue.
- *Increasing the transparency and efficiency of oil revenue mobilization and oil exploitation.* This would be especially beneficial for Chad because the government has no control over price volatility, and oil proceeds are likely to remain the main source of government revenue for the foreseeable future. Greater transparency and public involvement in oil revenue management could improve accountability and reduce elite capture. However, more remains to be done to improve the transparency and management of the sector. For example, the government needs to create a special commission for oil revenue monitoring that is both politically and socially inclusive.

- *Increasing competition in oil and mining exploration and production markets.* The government should consider reforming its oil and mining licensing policy, which has so far relied on the first-come, first-served principle, without actively promoting prospective acreage. Current investors are either large corporations that control all the production in the country or very small companies that appear undercapitalized and are not aggressively pursuing activities on their blocks. Targeted licensing and promotional strategies—coupled with improved sector oversight capacity—are needed to foster further development of the sector and ensure acreage turnover and activity (World Bank 2019b).

ACHIEVING ADEQUATE MACROFISCAL MANAGEMENT AND A BUSINESS-FRIENDLY ENVIRONMENT

The lack of fiscal space is a big challenge to achieve fiscal sustainability in the coming years. Chad is no longer benefiting from the substantial oil windfall revenue it did between 2008 and 2014, and the fiscal situation has been deteriorating under the COVID-19 pandemic. Oil revenues, by far the main source of public revenue, declined as a share of total revenues from 63.8 percent in 2005–14 to 36.9 percent in 2015–19, and are projected to fall further in the coming years. The country's fiscal policy stance has largely been procyclical. Procyclicality, coupled with the absence of a fiscal anchor, has resulted in insufficient public savings for policies aimed at stabilizing the economy and achieving intergenerational equity. The country's fiscal deficit (excluding grants) was significant and averaged 2.6 percent even during the oil price boom of 2005–14, before it widened to 3.4 percent in 2015–19. Chad's fiscal framework needs to be addressed to ensure its sustainability.

Strengthening non-oil revenue mobilization and implementing relevant PFM measures

To strengthen non-oil revenue mobilization and the implementation of relevant PFM measures, the authorities should consider the following:

- *Improving tools and policies for non-oil revenue mobilization.* Revenue collection remains low by regional and global standards. Low tax collection can be attributed to multiple factors, with the most prominent being weak tax administration, the large size of the Chadian informal sector, the proliferation of tax exemptions, a nonexistent value-added tax (VAT) refund mechanism, and a narrow VAT base resulting from the abundance of goods and services exempt from taxes or taxed at a reduced rate. Providing the tax administration with adequate physical and information technology (IT) infrastructure (building, furniture, IT system, and so on) and investing in HRM could ensure its adequate performance. Simplifying business registration processes and tax legislation, as well as improving transparency and accountability in the relationship between tax authorities and taxpayers, could contribute to efforts aimed at reducing the informal sector. Ensuring information sharing between the different administrations (tax, customs, land, and so on) through computerized processes would help broaden the tax base by identifying businesses not registered for tax purposes. To collect more revenues, the authorities need to implement a system that allocates a share of the VAT collected to refund needs, rationalize tax exemptions granted to businesses, and expand goods and services subject to VAT. Moreover, efforts are needed to improve the transparency, accountability, and efficiency of the customs administration to increase its contribution to domestic revenues.

- *Implementing a zero-tax bracket for the lowest incomes to both simplify revenue administration and enhance tax progressivity and equity.* The government needs to increase revenue in a way that does not increase the burden on the poor or impede the private sector's ability to create jobs. Rationalizing tax deductions is also needed, as they accrue disproportionally to the rich and lead to significant revenue losses. The use of digital tools would help the government make the tax and customs administrations and tax collection more efficient. Specific efforts need to be devoted to the transparency and efficiency of the customs administration to increase its contribution to public finances.
- *Ensuring that any fiscal reforms cover the public expenditure and procurement systems, given that Chad is currently struggling to achieve fiscal consolidation.* The government needs to pursue substantial reforms of the public expenditure system, including planning, budgeting, and spending. Specifically, it should (a) strengthen the budget planning process and establish a link between planning and budgeting, (b) improve its budget presentation to ease analysis by distinguishing between directly and indirectly productive sectors, (c) strengthen the public financial capacity and skills of some line ministries, and (d) reduce the use of special procedures in budget execution.
- *Reforming the public investment system, including in planning, budgeting, and implementation.* The government has taken considerable steps toward improving the efficiency and effectiveness of public investment management. For example, it created the Public Investment Management National Commission and improved the selection process for investment projects. However, further efforts are required to ensure the sustainability of PFM (budget preparation, execution, procurement, debt management), including (a) planning and coordinating investment decisions with all relevant institutions and (b) targeting the allocation of public resources and providing geographic coverage of the budget by department, municipality, and rural/urban area.
- *Reducing the risk of debt distress by achieving adequate debt restructuring and rationalizing public spending.* Chad is currently facing debt distress due to its high ratio of debt service to revenue. The government should implement the debt restructuring requested by bilateral and private creditors under the G20 common framework to reduce the risk level to moderate. Meanwhile, spending rationalization could be achieved through a prudent increase in current expenditures, improved payroll administration, and more efficient public investments. Significant weaknesses remain in debt transparency and management, despite improvements through reforms implemented in 2020. To improve debt transparency and management, the government should (a) create a consolidated and comprehensive database of debt contracts to enable better debt service monitoring and accurate and consistent data on the debt stock; (b) update and frequently maintain the current debt reporting system (Système informatisé de gestion et d'analyse de la dette, SYSGADE) for the timely provision of relevant reporting documents; (c) frequently publish debt bulletins with extensive coverage; (d) work toward debt restructuring to bring the debt risk to moderate; and (e) adopt a sustainable debt policy.

- *Improving integrity and transparency in the management of public resources to ensure the efficient execution of public procurement functions.* Despite the recent update of the Public Procurement Code to raise contract approval thresholds and ensure gender promotion, challenges remain. The authorities need to adopt meaningful reforms to improve the performance and efficiency of the public procurement system, including (a) implementing a transparent contract awarding system that uses a digital platform to limit direct contracting, (b) digitalizing procurement review and approval processes to reduce the time and cost required to complete the submission process, and (c) improving budget planning and implementation to avoid late payments and arrears that are likely to cause distortions and jeopardize public works companies and local banks.
- *Improving accountability for public spending by creating systematic transparency mechanisms and relying on citizen engagement to monitor the management of resources and effectiveness of services.* This could entail supporting proactive information disclosure on revenue, public expenditures, debt management, public procurement, and the performance of SOEs, as well as fostering citizen participation in PFM. Transparency mechanisms could be strengthened by improving annual performance reports/audits, transparency codes, asset declarations, citizen-state feedback loops, grievance mechanisms, and local community conflict resolution mechanisms.

Achieving regional integration and a business-friendly environment

In addition to insufficient infrastructure and weak development of human capital, Chad's private sector faces various trade and regulatory barriers. Data on Chad's business environment reveal that Chad underperforms most SSA countries on several indicators, including starting a business, dealing with construction permits, paying taxes, trading across borders, getting electricity, and getting credit. Moreover, private investment is highly constrained in the country by the high costs of labor and capital.[2] Meanwhile, lack of electricity is a major constraint on the development of the private sector in manufacturing and services.

To accelerate regional integration and create a business-friendly environment, the authorities should consider the following:

- *Strengthening economic integration with coastal and neighboring countries.* Chad should work with other countries in CEMAC (one of Africa's least integrated regions) to improve infrastructure, logistics, and regulation along the main regional trade corridors, with the aim to remove major bottlenecks to trade (such as illegal taxation and inefficient procedures/practices and border controls) and improve road quality. Regional integration should also be pursued with neighboring countries around Lake Chad to create an internal market covering northern Nigeria, northern Cameroon, Niger, and Chad. A well-functioning internal market could help to establish value chains that would, for example, integrate the livestock market with light manufacturing in meat and leather (for example, shoes and bags) processing.
- *Leveraging public policies and resources to crowd in private investment and reduce risk to boost the country's economic transformation.* Chad's economic

transformation requires an improvement in productivity and competitiveness, which could be achieved by increasing access to electricity, transport, and finance. In comparison to many other peers, and despite the creation of a presidential council, Chad lacks a coordinating mechanism dedicated to promoting a business-friendly environment. The government could increase the confidence of the private sector by setting up a strong public-private dialogue framework and improving the rule of law to ensure fairness.

- *Accelerating the adoption and implementation of business-friendly reforms already validated but that have been pending since 2017.* Measures that level the playing field for private investors will enhance growth by reducing the costs of entry and the barriers from having created "preferred" investors. These reforms include (a) improving the code of civil, commercial, and social procedures; (b) reforming the construction permit process; (c) improving the performance of the one-stop shop for starting a business to reduce the time and cost required to register; and (d) reducing the high number of tax payments and social contributions. In addition, sector-specific reforms are necessary to stimulate productivity and private investment. Energy; technology, media, and telecommunications; and information and communication technologies are important for the industrialization and modernization of the Chadian economy. Policy reforms in these sectors should focus on tariffs, regulation, the efficiency of public enterprises, and open access to competition.
- *Improving the availability of economic data and facilitating internal (between services) and external (with development partners) coordination on development projects and service delivery.* Access to quality data is essential for both designing and implementing economic policies. Meanwhile, internal and external coordination would ensure that decentralization efforts achieve the World Bank's twin goals and Chad's overreaching socioeconomic developmental objectives.

NOTES

1. Only policy actions that can have an impact within the next five years were included.
2. The World Economic forum ranked Chad last in terms of competitiveness (140th out of 140 countries) in 2019.

REFERENCES

World Bank. 2018a. "Escaping Chad's Growth Labyrinth: Disentangling Constraints from Opportunities and Finding a Path to Sustainable Growth." World Bank, Washington, DC. https://elibrary.worldbank.org/doi/pdf/10.1596/30941.

World Bank. 2018b. "Project Appraisal Document on a Proposed Grant to the Republic of Chad for a Refugees and Host Communities Support Project." World Bank, Washington, DC. http://documents.worldbank.org/curated/en/658761536982256019/pdf/PAD2809-PAD-PUBLIC-disclosed-9-12-2018-IDA-R2018-0286-1.pdf.

World Bank. 2019a. "Chad Public Expenditure Analysis: Fiscal Space for Productive Social Sectors Expenditure." World Bank, Washington, DC. https://openknowledge.worldbank.org/handle/10986/34616.

World Bank. 2019b. "Chad Petroleum Sector Diagnostic Report." February 2019. World Bank, Washington, DC. https://openknowledge.worldbank.org/bitstream/handle/10986/33898/Chad-Petroleum-Sector-Diagnostic-Report.pdf.

World Bank. 2019c. "Chad—Second Programmatic Economic Recovery and Resilience Development Policy Financing Project." World Bank, Washington, DC. https://documents.worldbank.org/en/publication/documents-reports/documentdetail/428811579575639441/chad-second-programmatic-economic-recovery-and-resilience-development-policy-financing-project.

World Bank. 2020. "Chad Petroleum Sector SME Competitiveness and Global Value Chains Upgrading Diagnostics." December. https://operationsportalws.worldbank.org/Pages/DocumentProfile.aspx?projectid=P166399&DocId=47&IsCovGen=true&removePublic=false&stage=AUS.

4 Key Pathways

OVERVIEW

To boost inclusive economic growth and create jobs, the government should focus on policy reforms and investments to improve public service delivery, close infrastructure gaps, and enable private sector development. The country should invest in accelerating the accumulation of human capital, with a focus on closing the gender gap, so that girls and women can contribute their full potential. It should also invest in productive infrastructure—including in energy, information and communication technologies, water, and transport and logistics—to improve connectivity and boost regional integration. Developing job-creating economic sectors in which the country has a strategic advantage, such as commercial agriculture and livestock, and emerging sectors, such as digital economy, will be key to support economic inclusion.

STRENGTHEN HUMAN CAPITAL AND REDUCE THE GENDER GAP

To reverse the recent setback in poverty reduction and build the foundation to change the medium-term trajectory of growth and poverty reduction, efforts are needed to mitigate shocks and increase Chad's human capital accumulation. Specifically, the government should address weak access to education and health care (through better, more targeted, and efficient public financing); low levels of women's inclusion in the economy; and low access to formal employment—all of which are binding constraints identified in chapter 2. In addition, the authorities need to reform the social protection system to ensure greater equity and accelerate the accumulation of human capital.

Improving access to and the quality of education and vocational training

To improve access to and the quality of education and vocational training, the authorities should consider the following:

- *Prioritizing strengthening human resources in the education sector.* This reform could be achieved by establishing a management policy for community teachers, improving teacher training, and creating clear criteria for human resource allocation, including toward underserved areas and marginalized population groups. It should also implement an incentive scheme that provides a package of accommodation and facilitates career progression for teachers serving in remote, conflict-affected, or at-risk areas that takes into account safety considerations. The authorities also need to formulate a clear strategy to support the payment of subsidies of level 1 and 2 community teachers to ensure the continuity of learning. Primary education is strongly dependent on community teachers, who represent about 67 percent of the teaching staff. Following the decision of the government to stop subsidizing community teachers, more than 2,000 primary schools closed, and the number of enrolled students fell by at least 250,000 between 2014 and 2017. Since 2018, Chad's technical and financial partners, including the World Bank, have helped to reopen schools and increase the enrollment rate, but this reliance on external support is unsustainable.
- *Increasing nonsalary budget expenditures is another high priority.* This reform is important to improve learning outcomes while improving the ability to track and monitor external resources and performance. It is also vital for strengthening governance through increased involvement of parents and communities in monitoring education outcomes and making schools accountable for results. Student learning conditions could be improved by building, rehabilitating, and renovating classrooms, and equipping schools with relevant tools.
- *Improving significantly the governance of the education sector.* This reform could be done by introducing and using objective criteria for the recruitment, allocation, and promotion of teachers and teaching staff, and it would require strong monitoring of investment in education and vocational training infrastructure and equipment. Efforts to improve the quality of governance in the education sector also need to address regional equality in the distribution of human resources, infrastructure, and equipment in primary, secondary, and tertiary education as well vocational training. To strengthen vocational training, a strong partnership with the private sector is key in terms of curriculum development, teacher training, student internships, and institutional management. Vocational training institutions need more autonomy while also being accountable for results (for example, through the establishment of a performance-based contract between the institutions and the ministry).
- *Adopting a classroom-based integrated approach to reduce the current high rate of learning poverty.* To address high learning poverty in Chad, the authorities need to ensure that (a) teachers are in class and teach, and students are in class and learn in a language they understand;[1] (b) teaching practice is improved and adjusted at the right level for students; (c) learning materials are available and used; and (d) teachers are continuously monitored, supported, and coached. The establishment of coherent curricula covering all levels of education, including scientific and technical education, is also key to improve the quality and relevance of education in Chad.
- *Implementing policies aimed at improving education outcomes and equity.* The structure of the education system is internally inefficient, yielding high dropout rates that increase by grade. The government could address equity issues by (a) reviewing the current scholarship program to target low-income

students; (b) raising awareness of social and cultural barriers to girls' access to primary, secondary, and higher education as well as technical and vocational education and training; and (c) setting up pro-poor policy programs focused on marginalized communities. The involvement of communities is a prerequisite to maintain children in school and improve learning outcomes.
- *Strengthening the education system to accommodate education in emergency settings, psychosocial support, and children with special needs.*[2] The education sector is under pressure due to the expanding school-age population and the increase in humanitarian crises in and outside the country that has led to population displacement. In Chad, about 52 percent of primary-age children are out of school (54 percent of girls and 50 percent of boys). A large proportion of out-of-school children, mainly in the eastern and western provinces, suffer from malnutrition, and many school districts host refugees from neighboring regions. These challenges require the adoption and reinforcement of an integrated and inclusive approach to education and learning in Chad.
- *Aligning the education and training system with the needs of the labor market and the private sector*. Prioritizing labor-intensive sectors of the economy is critical. Aware of the economic development potential of investments in science, technology, engineering, and mathematics, the government recruited more than 1,400 secondary school science teachers in 2019, which is a good starting point. However, the authorities need to consult extensively with the private sector, civil society organizations, and education partners to ensure consistency in the education and training system and its effective responsiveness to the labor market. Skills development is especially relevant for informal operators that are solicited by companies operating in the formal sector. Vocational programs in urban areas should be prioritized to promote future growth, and they should focus on urban service requests and new businesses to diversify the economy and leverage the introduction of new technologies. This is important because most new jobs come from urban activities and require significant skilled labor. Meanwhile, the government should empower and support people who complete their training in their professional and social integration, as this will encourage young people to attend vocational training and boost entrepreneurship.

Improving the performance of the health care system

Improving the performance of the country's health care system will require efforts across the health sector. The following recommendations address reforms that have the highest potential to expedite progress toward universal health coverage and improve human capital outcomes:

- *Strengthening the performance of the health sector to increase the coverage and quality of essential health services is critical.* This reform will require developing the health workforce (for example, mobilizing additional human resources and improving skills of staff already on the payroll); equipping health centers and addressing supply chain challenges; improving the coordination and supervision of community health workers to increase the coverage of community-based service delivery; strengthening routine data collection and reporting; and addressing demand-side barriers to access. In turn, these improvements will require additional financial resources to increase the budget for the maintenance of current infrastructure and health equipment, which would entail an increase in the public health budget. It is therefore critical to strengthen coordination within the Ministry of Health and between the finance and planning directorates in the budget preparation process while monitoring allocative and technical efficiency.

- *Prioritizing the training of additional health workers, improving in-service training, and deploying more staff in underserved areas.*[3] Health service delivery has historically suffered from a lack of critical inputs and inadequate staffing at district hospitals and health centers. The fragility of Chad's health system is aggravated by geographical and social factors. Ensuring that health centers have the resources to effectively deploy newly recruited health workers will increase the provision of health services both in N'Djamena and, especially, in rural and conflict-affected areas. Deploying health workers in rural, hard-to-reach, and conflict-affected regions will help to address regional imbalances and the lack of a positive state presence in these areas. As such, it will contribute to addressing exclusion among underserved population groups, which acts as a fragility driver that can increase the risk of conflict and violence.

- *Improving service delivery and leveraging technology and innovation.* Given Chad's low population density and poor transport infrastructure, it will be important to combine effective health promotion and prevention at the community level with quality health service delivery at the facility level. Community-based service delivery should be done in collaboration with traditional leaders and influential stakeholders in the community, and it should include awareness raising and behavioral change activities targeted at increasing the demand for essential health and nutrition services. Digital solutions could be leveraged to increase the coverage of essential services and address some of the most salient barriers to access (for example, geographic and financial barriers). Digital solutions could be used to deliver specialized care in underserved areas, given Chad's low number of specialized doctors. For instance, the use of mHealth and eHealth tools could allow a specialized doctor in N'Djamena to service remote areas throughout the country.

- *Improving the efficiency and efficacy of health financing and the environment for private investments in health care.*[4] Additional health investments are needed to improve the performance of the health sector and achieve the government's vision for the sector. The government should scale up health financing reforms targeted at improving the efficiency of health financing, including adopting performance-based financing. This would require public financial management (PFM) reforms to adapt the budgeting and planning process and promote greater transparency and accountability in the use of public funds. The government of Chad should ensure the effective implementation of the Free Health Care policy that grants free access to care for mothers and for children under five years old. Finally, the government needs to adopt relevant regulation and reduce administrative bottlenecks to create a more conducive environment for private sector investment in health care to increase the range of health services.

- *Strengthening pandemic preparedness and the health system's capacity to respond to pandemics, including COVID-19.* Recurring outbreaks of preventable diseases and epidemics in west Africa highlight the importance of strong disease surveillance and response systems. Chad should scale up its efforts to roll out the District Health Information Software 2 (DHIS2)[5] to allow the authorities to reliably collect epidemiological data in a timely way. Furthermore, a network of laboratories needs to be developed to promote synergies and improve the safety and quality of laboratory procedures. In addition, Chad should strengthen routine immunization programs and disease surveillance at the community level to prevent the occurrence of and quickly identify potential outbreaks.

Enhancing social protection programs

Chad's social protection system consists mostly of interventions that address cyclical and severe food insecurity, with limited programs that target long-term development and protection. However, over the past few years, the government has made significant efforts to create a more coordinated, long-term, and efficient social protection system that includes development and humanitarian partners and a focus on peripheral areas. Such a system seeks to harmonize efforts to avoid overlap and work toward increasing coverage and reach. The COVID-19 pandemic has highlighted the necessity and opportunities to improve the resilience of the social protection system and develop mechanisms that can rapidly provide income support to people in a crisis. Delivery systems could be made more robust and adaptive, with the capacity to deliver support faster and to more people, by incorporating unique and universal identification, social registries of poor and vulnerable households, and electronic/digital payment mechanisms that are also adapted to internally displaced persons (IDPs).

To continue the government's work to create a more coordinated, long-term, and efficient social protection system, the authorities should consider the following:

- *Increasing investment in social protection and service delivery systems to expand coverage.* First, the authorities should prioritize efforts to expand existing programs to the whole country,[6] increase the coverage of the poor in safety net programs, extend retirement and old-age savings systems to most formal sector workers, and allow informal workers to access the social protection system. Second, they should invest in more adaptive delivery systems, including effective early warning systems, a social registry, digital payment systems, and scalable safety net programs to respond to crises like COVID-19. Third, the authorities need to increase access to economic opportunities for and the productivity of vulnerable households, informal businesses, and microenterprises, as the pandemic has severely affected both formal and informal labor markets. For example, the crisis has delayed progress in adopting legislation granting unemployment benefits according to clearly stated criteria as a response to crises. Finally, the government needs to scale up (a) human capital investments in education and early childhood development to protect the current generation and improve access to social infrastructure (for example, schools and health centers) and (b) interventions to promote human capital development, including nutrition and early childhood stimulation.
- *Enhancing the coordination of safety net programs.* There is a need to improve coordination between the implementing agency Cellule Filets Sociaux and the Ministry of Social Affairs. There is also a need to strengthen governance and institutions to ensure proper implementation of programs and policies by deconcentrating services to avoid the centralization of safety net interventions within Cellule Filets Sociaux. The capacity of the government to appropriate the existing safety net system and secure funding through a budgetary or fiscal mechanism needs to be strengthened to ensure the sustainable implementation of social protection programs.

Empowering women and accelerating the demographic transition

Policy efforts to promote greater inclusion of women in Chad's economy must address all areas where barriers to gender equality persist, from influencing norms to ensuring equal access to opportunities. The specific challenges faced by women and girls in conflict-affected parts of the country should also be considered. To generate change, the authorities need to adopt gender-based policies that are ambitious and address barriers to implementation of reforms. Closing gender gaps requires legal changes and programs to influence social and cultural practices. To empower women and accelerate the demographic transition, the authorities should consider the following:

- *Ensuring that gender-based policies help improve learning outcomes, keep girls in school, and prevent teen pregnancies to reduce the gender gap for adolescents.* This reform could be achieved by (a) adopting scripted lesson plans and teaching at the right level to address girls' lower learning outcomes; (b) implementing programs designed to end child marriage, prevent early childbearing, and educate girls to empower adolescent girls; and (c) expanding skills development to offer an alternative to early family formation and improve the productivity of girls who have dropped out of school. Moreover, gender-based policies could include efforts to keep girls in school, help them return to school, or directly delay marriage while enforcing existing laws prohibiting female genital mutilation and early marriage as well as adopting community-led approaches to change gender norms.
- *Fully implementing the current legal framework to reduce gender-based violence, which has recently been on the rise.* Women's economic opportunities should be improved through better maternal health care, skills development, and better access to markets and productive assets. To reduce maternal mortality, the entire health care system needs to be functional, and women need folic acid before pregnancy, access to antenatal visits and services that can identify potentially dangerous conditions, institutionalized delivery, and functioning hospitals. In addition, women need greater access to and autonomy in reproductive health care. The implementation of Law N.06-2002 will be crucial to ensure women's autonomy in exercising their right to access health services. These reforms could help Chad reap the benefits of the demographic dividend. Behavioral change campaigns that increase women's autonomy and the demand for family planning should be tailored to the specific sociocultural characteristics of the country's diverse society and include an active engagement at the community level.
- *Improving women's skills and ensuring women have better access to inputs to close the gender gap in agriculture, entrepreneurship, and wage earnings.* Legislation needs to be amended to remove impediments to women's employment and entrepreneurship as well as access to various institutions. Women need to be involved in the decisions related to the response to the COVID-19 crisis, and women and girls need to be deliberately targeted in all efforts made to address the pandemic (World Bank 2021).
- *Ensuring that polices that promote greater inclusion of women also cover vulnerable groups such as people with disabilities.* The national program for women empowerment that is currently under preparation should also address the needs of youth and vulnerable groups that also face constraints in terms of access to economic opportunities. There is also a need to create

a bank to increase the productivity of needy families (including households with members living with a handicap) and low-income households and integrate them into the society.

IMPROVE INFRASTRUCTURE FOR BETTER SERVICE DELIVERY

Chad needs to both build and maintain key energy, water, transport, and telecommunications infrastructure to improve access to basic services. A strategic and holistic approach to infrastructure development is needed to improve the efficiency of public service delivery, including in marginalized areas. Chad needs to find a sustainable way to finance new and maintain existing infrastructure. The authorities should focus on improving the management and oversight of SOEs to ensure effective and efficient service delivery and that they contribute effectively to infrastructure development.[7] This reform will require the contribution of the private sector, and the government may need to rely on public-private partnerships to improve the quality of public service delivery. Regardless, the authorities need to focus on the quality of infrastructure in terms of metrology, standardization, and conformity, as well as how to make investments resilient to evolving climate impacts. Priority should be given to energy and transport infrastructure in the short to medium terms.

Reforming the energy sector to improve access

Chad's energy sector is facing two major related challenges: inadequate access to electricity and an inefficient supply of electricity.

Significantly increasing access to electricity would require massive efforts to increase power generation and import/export capacity, extend and strengthen the transmission and distribution power grid, and deploy off-grid solutions at scale. Given the time required to implement on-grid electrification, the nascent state of the national power grid (which is limited to the capital city of N'Djamena), and the low population density in rural areas that accommodate nearly three-fourths of the country's population, mini-grids and stand-alone solar systems (SSS) are poised to play a significant role in providing access to electricity through 2030. Mini-grids will need to be implemented in secondary cities, and SSS will be needed in rural and peripheral areas to provide electricity access to productive uses, public entities, and households. Mini-grid and SSS solutions can be deployed relatively quickly and can function as pre-electrification in locations that will be connected to the national power grid. Integral attention also needs to be paid to customer services and the inclusion of marginalized groups. The national grid is expected to reach some scale in the second part of this decade, supported by the construction of the high-voltage transmission line connecting the power systems of Chad and Cameroon under the World Bank–supported Cameroon-Chad Power Interconnection Project.

Ensuring the efficiency of the electricity supply is a key prerequisite for making the electricity sector sustainable, ensuring a reliable electricity supply, and increasing electricity access. The electricity supply in N'Djamena and a dozen secondary cities, which is served by small mini-grids, has been inefficient due the high cost of generation, large commercial losses, low payment collection, loss-making tariffs, and poor operational performance. A reform program to address these issues will need to include the following measures:

- *Reducing the cost of power generation* by (a) switching from diesel to heavy fuel oil in existing thermal plants owned by the national power utility Société Nationale d'Electricité (SNE) and independent power producers; (b) procuring new generation capacity through competitive and transparent tenders; (c) using petroleum gas, which is currently flared, for power generation; (d) increasing the share of cost-effective renewable solar energy and storage while optimizing dispatching; and (e) importing competitively priced electricity.
- *Reducing inefficiencies in the distribution and sale of electricity* by implementing a revenue protection program to address commercial losses and improve payment collections.
- *Enhancing the governance of SNE* by implementing a performance contract between the government and SNE. The contract would specify (a) SNE's services and operational indicators, (b) the level of public subsidies needed if tariffs fail to cover costs, and (c) government obligations for the payment of electricity bills by public and parastatal entities.[8]
- *Developing further a legal and regulatory framework* to (a) create the foundation for the financially viable operation of SNE and mini-grids operated by the private sector by establishing cost-reflective tariffs and (b) promote private sector participation, which is hampered by SNE's chronic loss-making operations and its deficient legal status (especially in terms of the ownership of energy assets).

The objective of the engagement of the World Bank Group in the energy sector in the coming years should include (a) boosting energy access, (b) enhancing the governance of the sector governance, (c) diversifying the energy mix to reduce cost and emissions, and (d) improving the operational and financial viability of the national power utility (SNE) (table 4.1).

Improving transport infrastructure and logistics services

To improve the country's transport infrastructure and logistics services, the authorities should consider the following:

- *Addressing the country's poor transport infrastructure and service delivery to connect marginalized areas and population groups.* This reform can be done by (a) developing multimodal corridor networks, (b) improving trade and border-crossing services, and (c) improving operational and institutional effectiveness. The first two priorities can be addressed through regional integration investment programs financed by the government, with support from donors.
- *Focusing on road asset management to improve operational and institutional effectiveness.* Chad faces challenges in meeting the required financial and technical requirements to maintain its road network. To address these challenges, the authorities first need access to dedicated and secured resources for road maintenance. The Road Fund has shrunk over the past five years due to fiscal constraints. To ensure the Road Fund is properly funded, and to restore donor confidence in the government's ability to maintain transport investments, the authorities need to review the governance of the Road Fund and adopt rules to ensure its proper functioning and accountability.

TABLE 4.1 **The World Bank Group's energy program in Chad**

Objective	DPF and related TA	Chad Energy Access Scale-up MPA	Cameroon-Chad Interconnection Project	ROGEP	IFC and MIGA
(1) Increase access to electricity	National electrification analysis **(MPE)**	Electrification of N'Djamena, secondary city, and rural areas	Electrification of N'Djamena and locations along the HV transmission line	Support to the private sector for SSS electrification	• Financing private sector • PRG • Political risk insurance for solar projects
(2) Enhance sector governance	• Performance contract • Auditing financial statements **(SNE)**	n.a.	n.a.	n.a.	n.a.
(3) Diversify the energy mix to reduce costs and emissions	• Least-cost development plan • Switching from diesel to HFO • Competitive procurement of new generation capacity	Hybridizing grids in N'Djamena and secondary cities by leveraging private capital in solar PV and storage	Electricity imports from Cameroon	n.a.	• Containerized solar PV and storage • Scaling mini-grid program • Political risk insurance for solar projects
(4) Improve performance of SNE	• Tariff methodology **(ARSE)** • Revenue Protection Program (RPP) **(SNE)**	Implementation of RPP in N'Djamena and secondary cities	Implementation of RPP in N'Djamena	n.a.	n.a.

Source: World Bank staff proposal.
Note: ARSE = Autorité de Régulation du Secteur de l'Energie, the energy regulatory body; DPF = Development Policy Financing; HFO = heavy fuel oil; HV = high voltage; IFC = International Finance Corporation (of the World Bank Group); MIGA = Multilateral Investment Guarantee Agency (of the World Bank Group); MPA = Multiphase Programmatic Approach; MPE = Ministry of Petroleum and Energy; n.a. = not applicable; PRG = partial risk guarantee; PV = photovoltaic; ROGEP = Regional Off-Grid Electricity Access Project; RPP = Revenue Protection Program; SSS = stand-alone solar system; SNE = Société Nationale d'Electricité (national power utility); TA = technical assistance.

- *Outsourcing road maintenance to the private sector to address operational inefficiencies.* There is a global trend to transfer road maintenance from in-house public entities to the private sector through predefined arrangements called performance-based contracts or output-based contracts for road maintenance. Performance-based contracts have proven to be effective in reducing costs, improving road conditions, and delivering transport services.
- *Developing better funding mechanisms in the transport sector to achieve sustained improvements to transportation infrastructure.* Currently, infrastructure projects and the maintenance of existing infrastructure are funded by the national government, with external support from donors. However, these funding sources have proven inadequate to meet the country's transportation needs. In 2000, a specific fund was established solely for road maintenance, and it was intended to generate approximately US$19 million per year through a fuel tax. The resources accrued by the fund would be used to maintain approximately 7,500 kilometers of primary roads. However, the fund has failed to meet its goal due to low levels of collected resources, issues with the funds being transferred, and the exclusion of rural communities.

Improving the efficiency of the water sector

The government needs to prioritize the implementation of reforms in the water sector, focusing both on the access and quality of services and on customer experiences. To address the challenges facing the sector, the authorities should consider the following:

- *Strengthening the institutions and governance of the water sector.* The ministry responsible for water, and the government more broadly, needs to be equipped with the necessary instruments for piloting, regulating, and managing the sector, spanning from water resources management to various water services (for example, drinking water, water for agriculture, water for ecosystems regeneration, and so on). The instruments need to contribute to a more efficient geographical and subsectoral targeting of external support, which remains poorly managed.
- *Ensuring appropriate management of water resources.* The management and regulation of the use of ground and surface water need to be reinforced at both central and local government levels. Although some monitoring equipment exists in the country, most is not maintained, and water resources (availability, quality, and variability) are not monitored. Due to mounting pressure, both socioeconomic and from climate change, proper monitoring and management of water resources are becoming paramount. The characterization of the all type of uses is important to define and clarify taxation to apply the principles of the polluter-pays and user-pays rules to ensure the sustainability of water resource management (water security).
- *Ensuring the sustainable financing of the Chadian Water Company (Société Tchadienne des Eaux, STE).* Improving the performance of urban hydraulics is dependent on the financial recovery of STE. A project under preparation, which is receiving funding from the Dutch Development Cooperation, the French Development Agency, and the European Union, includes institutional support for STE and investments in N'Djamena. However, other STE centers require urgent investments to restore service to some of the country's largest cities. The government could consider the taxation of water abstraction to fund STE.
- *Implementing management models for water systems in semi-urban centers.* There is an ongoing discussion on the proper management models for small-piped water systems in semi-urban centers and the envisaged evolution toward medium-size *affermage* contracts with private operators. The implementation of a properly managed model should be combined with technical assistance to help define the reforms and investments needed to develop or rehabilitate small urban water systems, including flood protection. The government could pilot different forms of management or technologies (for example, solar) aimed at reducing operating costs and promoting social connections.
- *Designing and implementing a rural water strategy to strengthen the planning, monitoring, and regulation of the water sector.* A rural water strategy is also needed to expand and rehabilitate water supply infrastructure, with a focus on peripheral and conflict-affected or at-risk areas and the inclusion of marginalized population groups. The strategy should include options to secure water for irrigation, including by exploring ways to use water related to oil production for agricultural use. It should also focus on Lake Chad and the impact of climate change on livelihoods.

Expanding the telecommunications network

Several telecommunication regulations have been enacted over the past five years, with a limited impact on private sector investment. These regulations were meant to improve the competitiveness of the sector, but they mainly favored established operators. Limited access to and poor quality of digital connectivity continue to hamper Chad's ability to attract private investors to the telecommunications sector.

To expand the telecommunications network, the authorities should consider the following:

- *Opening the international gateway to competition, removing legal barriers to the creation of additional international gateways, and laying and using fiber cables to improve the quality and reach of telecommunication services.* This reform will require ensuring a level playing field between private operators and the state-owned provider, as well as the creation of a procompetition regulatory framework to enable the development of mobile money services that could strengthen financial inclusion and facilitate the inflow of remittances from abroad. The government could also promote contestability (that is, enabling the entry of a third mobile network operator) by (a) issuing wholesale broadband licenses; (b) issuing licenses for independent tower operators; (c) allowing internet service providers to be facilities based, including allocating spectrum for fixed wireless access; and (d) introducing specialized universal service operators. It should also institutionalize mobile money as a means of payment (for example, for the payment of taxes, bills, fines, or merchandise) and receiving social cash transfers or salaries. The authorities need to review taxation in the sector and strengthen the local regulator through a comprehensive regulatory technical assistance program.
- *Granting licenses to designated universal service operators, which is expected to increase mobile network investment in rural areas, increasing the availability of mobile internet services for both households and businesses.* The increase in licenses was expected to increase the geographic coverage of mobile broadband networks from 30 percent in 2019 to 45 percent by 2021. Moreover, enabling end users to switch providers and broadband operators to create mobile internet infrastructure would increase competition and reduce network rollout costs. This cost reduction would increase the service affordability and uptake of mobile internet. As a result, the number of unique mobile internet subscribers was expected to increase from 15 percent in 2019 to 20 percent in 2021.

PROMOTE DIVERSIFICATION AND SECTORS WITH JOBS POTENTIAL

Weak productivity and social return on economic activities in rural areas and low access to formal employment are key binding constraints on economic growth and poverty reduction. Chad could address these constraints by promoting sectors with a strategic advantage—such as agriculture, livestock, light manufacturing, digital economy, green economy, and microfinance sector—with a view to enhance economic opportunities in peripheral, conflict-affected, and at-risk areas. These sectors satisfy the following criteria: (a) revealed comparative advantage (RCA),[9] (b) potential trajectory of global demand, (c) employment elasticity, and (d) prospects for domestic value addition and economic diversification. The current and potential impact of climate change is also important in determining the strategic advantage of products and sectors. Chad boasts considerable opportunities for private sector investment in sectors that can drive structural transformation, notably in livestock, sesame seeds, and gum arabic, as well as cotton production—the historic cash crop.

According to the 2021 Country Private Sector Diagnostic (CPSD) (IFC 2021), Chad has high RCA in agricultural products as well as in the oil and the extractive sector. Over the past few years, only 11 of the country's agri-based products seem to have demonstrated RCA, and these include gum arabic, sesame, maize, raw cotton, woven fabrics, and fiber wadding. Based on the criteria for strategic advantage, agriculture and agro-processing appear to have high growth potential for Chad. The potential of livestock is also relevant, although it is difficult to compute the RCA due to data shortcomings. However, the livestock sector has traditionally been a strategic sector for Chad, as it has fueled the country's exports and been a source of livelihoods for a large segment of the population.

Increasing agricultural productivity and livestock exports and supporting light agro-processing

To improve the agriculture sector, the authorities should consider the following:

- *Encouraging private sector participation in key agricultural input markets and supporting climate-smart agricultural practices.* This reform would boost agricultural productivity, which has been subdued due to low use of seeds and fertilizers. The government could also adopt policies to promote water conservation by (a) regulating freshwater abstraction for industrial uses and (b) promoting the use of water produced in petroleum operations to support agricultural irrigation and other industries.
- *Ensuring sustained productivity growth in agriculture through technological innovation.* This reform would depend on the timely availability of improved inputs such as seeds, fertilizer, and crop chemicals. Stimulating the development of an efficient, profitable, and competitive fertilizer industry will require a two-pronged approach to strengthen the demand for and supply of fertilizer. Demand for fertilizer is currently very weak in Chad, which means that efforts to improve the supply will be unsuccessful unless they are accompanied by activities to increase effective demand. Farmers should be trained and supported in the use of technology and improved inputs. The use of digital technologies could be promoted by adopting an e-extension approach, including the use of call centers, smartphones, and tablets to disseminate agricultural information.
- *Formulating a national land policy to increase agricultural productivity.* Chad needs to develop a national land policy for the effective, sustainable, and equitable use of land for social development and economic growth. As access to land, water, and other natural resources is at the heart of increasing intercommunal conflicts in the country, the national land policy will not only need to ensure it does not exacerbate risks but also seek to strengthen the rights of the various land users. An efficient land policy would allow for the formulation of appropriate land reforms and laws and the development and implementation of strategies, programs, and projects to facilitate stable and sustainable development. However, it is unlikely that the ongoing process to review the draft land code would adequately renew Chad's overall land tenure system.
- *Adopting sector-specific policies to incentivize private investment.* In terms of sesame and gum arabic value chains, the government should (a) invest in

quality grading, a traceability system, and forestry management, working through exporter and trader associations; (b) divert some subsidies for cotton exports to sesame to promote the use of fertilizer, certified seeds, or herbicides, potentially using e-vouchers, to promote the resilience of farmers through the diversification of their crop portfolio; (c) exempt traders from taxes in multiple cantons when transiting goods; (d) invest in sorting facilities at key trading points, working through exporter and farmer associations; and (e) support the professionalization of the value chain through collective action. In terms of the cotton value chain, it critical to deregulate the market for cotton by allowing competition to CotonTchad, with a view to enhance competition and strengthen the bargaining power of farmers.

- *Ensuring the livestock reform agenda focuses on policies that protect the supply chain, from production sites to trade corridors, border crossings, and destination markets.* Some of these policies are health related and pertain to sanitary procedures, while others focus on protecting production and trade processes. Stakeholders should be organized to reduce the number of intermediaries between producers and end traders along the value chain. Private investment should also be encouraged to modernize production infrastructure and enhance the local transformation and productivity of products. To achieve this, the government should (a) implement regional regulations on livestock such as enforcing animal passports and veterinary services for animal health, (b) reduce waiting times at customs by expanding posts and modernizing/digitalizing the customs process, and (c) develop a general map of the livestock sector and a livestock export-processing map to identify key bottlenecks along the value chain. To improve health inspections and veterinary services, the authorities need to expand and train a network of veterinary assistants and ensure the quality of imported veterinary pharmaceuticals. Most importantly, the government should invest in cold chain infrastructure and temperature-controlled logistics services and promote the use of quality standards and certification to move from exporting live cattle to exporting breeding products.
- *Supporting light manufacturing—mainly in the leather, cotton, and milk industries—to diversity the economy.* Although many of the products in these industries are bulky and thus expensive to transport for a country with poor infrastructure such as Chad, there is a market for these products in neighboring countries. Chad's geographic location in central Africa is also an advantage in positioning the country as a regional manufacturing hub.[10]

Supporting the digital economy, increasing access to credit, and promoting digital payments

To support the digital economy, increase access to credit, and promote digital payments, the authorities should consider the following:

- *Bridging the digital divide between urban, semi-urban, rural, and marginalized areas and population groups, as well as between men and women, to ensure inclusive growth and economic development.* Chad should continue to extend the use of digital connectivity technologies across the country through three key stages, to be carried out in parallel (Decoster 2019):
  - Stage 1. Chad ensures an institutional framework conducive to collaboration and dialogue between all stakeholders, makes all market data

available, and strengthens the transparency and efficiency of institutional agencies.
- Stage 2. Chad ensures an institutional framework that promotes private investment in the digital economy by (a) lowering entry barriers for new innovative firms through a flexible system of authorizations and licenses, (b) reducing costs with the facilitation of rights of way, (c) ensuring the effective functioning of the wholesale market for international capacity with the commissioning of fiber to Sudan, (d) establishing an internet exchange point, and (e) ensuring taxation is conducive to private sector development.
- Stage 3. Chad considers a major investment plan aimed at supporting the extension of digital connectivity through the allocation of public subsidies to close the digital divide in remote and rural areas suffering from persistent market failure (that is, absence of private operators due to very low profitability).

- *Boosting digital connectivity such as restructuring the incumbent SOE (Sotel) and introducing a wholesale open access model.* This reform includes fostering competition by enabling the entry of a third mobile network operator—MNO (for example, by issuing a license for independent tower operators, allowing internet service provider—ISPs—to be facilities-based, and introducing specialized user services platforms—USPs); and reducing the cost of digital connectivity by promoting infrastructure sharing (for example, wholesale broadband licenses) and reviewing taxation in the information and communication technology sector.
- *Addressing the structural weaknesses in Chad's financial landscape that have been highlighted by the COVID-19 crisis.* This reform could help the country rebuild better, with improved access to credit and financial inclusion. A more digitized financial system, with mobile money as a key driver, could increase the financial inclusion of marginalized groups and improve productivity by reducing transaction costs and spurring innovation. In a geographically vast country with security challenges, digital financial services can play important economic, social, and even security-related roles.
- *Designing and efficiently implementing key policies aimed at improving access to finance and financial inclusion.* Such policies must (a) support the digitalization of financial services to improve competition and ensure interoperability and fair access to unstructured supplementary service data; (b) pursue the digitization of government payments (in and out) through digital platforms that integrate mobile payments involving, for example, salaries, transfers, and taxes; (c) support the creation of a property registry to reduce the time and cost of registering a property; (d) support the creation of a risk-sharing facility that provides partial guarantees to financial institutions to increase lending (by reducing the risk of the loans) to small and medium enterprises (with different windows); and (e) support the development of microfinance by addressing structural needs such as supervision and access to financial resources. Given that the regulation and supervision of multilateral microfinance institutions are done by the Ministry of Finance, the authorities need to promote the development of sustainable microfinance practices to develop the sector, which plays a unique role in serving the poorest households and enhancing public confidence in the entire financial system.

NOTES

1. This reform is in the early stages and will take time to become fully effective. Strong political, technical, and financial commitment will be required to stay the course.
2. Disabled children, undernourished children, young mothers, and so on.
3. The density of health personnel at the national level was estimated at 0.58 per 1,000 inhabitants in 2016, with stark regional disparities, which especially affects rural, hard-to-reach, and conflict-affected regions, where most vulnerable people live. By contrast, the WHO's standard to achieve the Millennium Development Goals for 2015 was 2.3 per 1,000 inhabitants (World Bank 2019).
4. The current level of public health financing is low, which hinders the implementation of reforms that promote improvements in human capital while posing a large financial burden on households.
5. DHIS2 is an open source, web-based platform often used as a health management information system (https://dhis2.org/about/).
6. Current coverage is for selected beneficiaries among host communities and refugees in the country's nine refugee-hosting areas and limited to the camps and surrounding 25 kilometers, although some extension into urban areas was provided as an exceptional measure to respond to COVID-19 in 2021. This coverage is supported through the World Bank Group–financed Refugees and Host Communities Support Project, with dedicated financing from the Window for Host Communities and Refugees.
7. By, for example, improving legislation and building the capacity of the Ministry of Finance and line ministers in terms of oversight, debt management, and transparency in the management of public establishments and SOEs.
8. Implementing the national energy emergence plan adopted in 2020 could be a first step.
9. RCA is based on Ricardian trade theory, which posits that patterns of trade among countries are governed by their relative differences in productivity. Although such productivity differences are difficult to observe, an RCA metric can be readily calculated using trade data to reveal such differences. The metric can be used to provide a general indication and first approximation of a country's competitive export strengths—without prejudice to applied national measures that affect competitiveness, such as tariff/nontariff measures, subsidies, and others. When a country has an RCA for a given product (RCA >1), it is inferred to be a competitive producer and exporter of that product relative to a country producing and exporting that good at or below the world average. A country with an RCA for a product is considered to have an export strength in that product. The higher the value of a country's RCA for that product, the higher its export strength is for that product.
10. See the 2021 CPSD for further details (IFC 2021).

REFERENCES

Decoster, X. 2019. "Note de politique sectorielle TICs au Tchad (P168380)." World Bank, Washington, DC. https://imagebank2.worldbank.org/search/31115117.

IFC (International Finance Corporation). 2021. "Creating Markets in Chad: Taking Advantage of All Your Potential, 2021 Country Private Sector Diagnostic (CPSD)." World Bank, Washington, DC.

World Bank. 2019. "Chad Public Expenditure Analysis: Fiscal Space for Productive Social Sectors Expenditure." World Bank, Washington, DC. https://openknowledge.worldbank.org/handle/10986/34616.

World Bank. 2021. "Chad: The Economic Benefits of a Post-COVID-19 Gender-Equitable Society." World Bank, Washington, DC. https://openknowledge.worldbank.org/handle/10986/36444.

5 Knowledge Gaps

The World Bank has been pursuing a substantial Advisory Services and Analytics (ASA) program to identify knowledge and data gaps since 2016. A Public Expenditure Review (PER) was completed in 2019, a Poverty Assessment and a Risk and Resilience Assessment (RRA) were completed in 2021, and a household survey to provide updated data on poverty indicators was carried out in 2018–19. Moreover, other Advisory Services and Analytics initiatives have been completed in education, gender, health, social protection, extractive industries, water, agriculture, environment, climate, risk and resilience, the financial sector, and procurement (table 5.1).

In the next five years, the World Bank plans to complete both a Country Economic Memorandum and a Country Climate and Development Report (CCDR) for the G5 Sahel.[1] It also aims to produce a new Poverty Assessment and a PER for Chad. The CCDR will explore developments through a climate lens to tackle climate change more effectively, and it will include a comprehensive study of the economics of climate change. The World Bank will also complete a Country Environment Analysis, with the objective to assist the government of Chad in understanding key environmental challenges that affect development and to recommend climate-resilient pathways to support capacity building, policy development, and investments for a green economy.

In addition, there will be efforts to increase the effectiveness of reforms and interventions in the energy sector. These efforts will require analytical work, including (a) a more detailed geographic information system mapping to identify priority areas for the main electricity grid, mini-grids, and solar home systems based on a demand analysis; (b) a survey on the ability and willingness of households to pay for electricity services; (c) mini-grid studies; (d) a least-cost generation plan based on economic principles; (e) an evaluation of the elements that could be included in the national electrification strategy; and (f) an evaluation of the elements of a revenue protection program based on a sound financial model. Moreover, the authorities need to (a) reform state-owned enterprises; (b) ensure better deployment of state resources across the country; (c) address the weak capacity of the public administration; (d) improve the performance of the civil service; and (e) develop a pragmatic approach to improve non-oil revenue mobilization.

TABLE 5.1 Advisory services and analytics in Chad, 2016–21

FY16–FY17 ASA	FY18 ASA		FY19 ASA			ASA planned for FY20 and FY21		
	Task ID	Lead GP / Global Themes	Task name	Task ID	Lead GP / Global Themes	Task name	Task ID	Lead GP / Global Themes	Task name

FY18 ASA			FY19 ASA			ASA planned for FY20 and FY21		
Task ID	Lead GP / Global Themes	Task name	Task ID	Lead GP / Global Themes	Task name	Task ID	Lead GP / Global Themes	Task name
P132615	Education	Education and Skills Development for Competitiveness in Chad	P164477	Poverty and Equity	Niger and Chad Poverty Program	P153910	Social Protection and Labor	Chad Country Program-Adaptative Social Protection
P156857	Energy and Extractives	Extractive Industries Transparency Initiative Post-Compliance	P166711	Social Protection and Labor	Chad Strengthening Social Protection Systems and Adapting Them to the Refugee Crisis	P165092	Education	Chad Service Delivery
P164426	Energy and Extractives	Chad Power Sector Note	P167723	Water	Chad Water Supply and Sanitation Sector Note	P166399	Energy and Extractives	Chad Petroleum Sector Diagnostic (Done)
P165292	Macroeconomics, Trade and Investment	Chad Growth Study	P168380	Digital Development	Chad ICT Sector Development	P169177	Governance	Chad Public Procurement Assessment Using MAPS II
			P168773	Macroeconomics, Trade and Investment	Chad Public Expenditure Review	P171550	Poverty	Poverty Assessment
			P168813	Finance Competitiveness and Innovation	Chad Financial Sector Note	P171690	Macroeconomics, Trade and Investment	Chad: The Economic Benefits of a Gender-Inclusive Society
						P167721	Agriculture	Rural Land Tenure and Agricultural Production System in Chad
						P168359	Social, Urban, Rural and Resilience	Chad: Operationalization of IDA Immediate Response Mechanism
						FY20	FCV	Risk and Resilience Assessment
						FY20	Macroeconomics, Trade and Investment	SCD

No ASA produced (FY16–FY17)

Source: World Bank.
Note: ASA = Advisory Services and Analytics; GP = Global Practice; ICT = information and communication technology; FCV = fragility, conflict, and violence; MAPS II = methodology assessing procurement systems II; SCD = Systematic Country Diagnostic.

Additional efforts are needed to close the data gap. Effective policy making to reduce poverty and boost shared prosperity requires credible information on the nature, extent, cause, and impact of poverty and inequality. Given rising insecurity, fragility, and conflict in Chad, this will also involve not only better integration of associated risks but also opportunities to support government efforts around conflict prevention and resilience. The collection of this information requires a well-functioning system to measure living standards, poverty, and inequality at the individual and societal levels. The authorities need to be able to compare the relative situation of socioeconomic groups and assess the impact of policy interventions on the target population. It is also important to ascertain whether poverty is largely chronic or transitory. This type of data system supports managing for results, a public sector management approach that uses information on performance and results to improve decision-making.

There is a need to strengthen the collection of sectoral and administrative data. Since 1973, the country has not conducted an agricultural census, which is essential to evaluate the agriculture sector and to project agricultural production based on a permanent agricultural survey. The latest livestock survey was done in 2014, which means it is unable to inform policy makers. In addition, the collection of data on the education, health, mining, and oil sectors, which is essential to monitor human capital accumulation, is hampered by the lack of funding and qualified staff.

There is also a need to extend data collection to new areas such as enterprises, electricity, digital technologies, fragility and violence, and infrastructure. Given Chad's large youth population, promoting the private sector is key to ensure jobs are available for new entrants to the labor market. However, the country lacks a permanent enterprise survey to track the evolution of formal and informal employment. This information gap needs to be filled to support the structural transformation of the economy. Similarly, there is no national household/enterprise survey designed to understand the demand and use of electricity and digital technologies, even though the lack of access to electricity is a key constraint on Chad's development, while digital technologies constitute an important economic opportunity. Fragility and conflict data also need to be systematically collected and integrated into other analytical work to help inform policy making and guide investments.

Chad needs to invest in developing innovative, cost-effective, and data-driven early warning systems that could inform decision-making in times of crisis. Each year, the country faces various seasonal shocks—such as malaria, floods, and food insecurity—that affect many households. However, the lack of early warning systems prevents the government from anticipating and proactively reacting to these events. The COVID-19 pandemic, which has had a big negative impact on households and the country's economy, has highlighted the importance of such systems. Phone-based High-Frequency Surveys, for instance, provide low-cost high-frequency data to monitor the impact of the COVID pandemic and inform program and policy responses.

There is also a scope to invest in leveraging recent innovations in the use of high-quality geospatial data and machine-learning techniques. The availability of affordable high-frequency and high-quality satellite imagery and geospatial data can help fill in data gaps on where people live, settlement and land use patterns, transport networks and travel times, and climate and other risks. This can also be complemented with linked and georeferenced administrative data on facility locations to credibly assess service gaps and objectively inform decisions about where to invest in new facilities and how to bring services closer to people, particularly those who live in rural and remote areas.

Finally, Chad needs to invest in a high-quality, citizen-generated data system. This will complement other data sources by mapping local infrastructure and community assets, and it will provide frequent feedback on the availability and quality of service delivery. Investing in additional and complementary sources of data will also help to inform the analytical work that is needed and designed to collectively identify effective development policies and interventions. This will help the authorities identify the footprint of the state (or lack thereof) across the country and build incentives for greater accountability, improving current analytical techniques that rely solely on low-frequency survey and census efforts.

NOTE

1. Burkina Faso, Chad, Mali, Mauritania, and Niger.

APPENDIX A

Benchmarks for Chad Systematic Country Diagnostic

TABLE A.1 Systematic Country Diagnostic benchmark list, Chad

COUNTRY GROUPS	NEIGHBORING COUNTRIES AND COUNTRIES IN KEY REGIONAL ORGANIZATIONS	ASPIRATIONAL PEERS
CEMAC	Burkina Faso	Botswana
FCS	Cameroon	Côte d'Ivoire
G5 Sahel	Central African Republic	Rwanda
Lower-income countries	Congo, Republic of	Senegal
Sub-Saharan Africa	Equatorial Guinea	
	Gabon	
	Libya	
	Mali	
	Niger	
	Nigeria	
	South Sudan	
	Sudan	

Source: World Bank.
Note: CEMAC = Economic and Monetary Community of Central Africa; FCS = Fragile and Conflict-Affected Situations; G5 Sahel = Burkina Faso, Chad, Mali, Mauritania, and Niger.

APPENDIX B

Stakeholders for Chad Consultations

TABLE B.1 Stakeholder consultations in Chad, September 13–17, 2021

NAME	TITLE	INSTITUTION
Government		
Aboubakar Adam Ibrahim	Director General of Economy	Ministry of Economy, Development Planning, and International Cooperation (MEPDCI)
Douzounet Mallaye	Director of Analysis and Prospective Studies	Ministry of Economy, Development Planning, and International Cooperation
Gadom Djal Gadom	Director of Strategies and Economic Policy	Ministry of Economy, Development Planning, and International Cooperation
Dobingar Allesembaye	Director General of Studies and Forecasting	Ministry of Economy, Development Planning, and International Cooperation
Saleh Idriss Goukouni	Director of Studies and Forecasting	Ministry of Finance and Budget
Oumar Lamana	Director of Planning	Ministry of Infrastructure and Opening Up
Allabaye Jean François	Head of Monitoring and Evaluation Division	Ministry of Infrastructure and Opening Up
Ziang Saint Leon	Project Monitoring and Unit Coordinator	Ministry of Infrastructure and Opening Up
Konodji GuelngarRoland	Technical Director General	Ministry of Post and Telecommunications
Banbo Dihoulne Tchoubobe	Director of Private Sector Promotion	Ministry of Trade and Industry
Martine Dangar	Secretary General	Ministry of Women Affairs, Family and Child Protection
Nadjwa Mahamat Abdel-Bagui	Deputy Director General	National Institute of Statistics, Economic and Demographic Studies
Ahmat Souleyman	Director of Economic Statistics	National Institute of Statistics, Economic and Demographic Studies
Noubadiguim Ronelyam Baye	Head of the Department of Demographic Studies and Cartography	National Institute of Statistics, Economic and Demographic Studies
Bou-Ah Ban-Orngue	Director of Information and IT Management and IT	National Institute of Statistics, Economic and Demographic Studies

continued

TABLE B.1 *continued*

NAME	TITLE	INSTITUTION
Technical and Financial Partners		
Guimsi Wilffrid	Resident Representative	Development Bank of the Central African States
Carton Didier	Acting Head of Delegation	European Union
Vingut Lorenzo	Good Governance Team Leader	European Union
Maracchi Nicolas	Infrastructure Team Leader	European Union
Kirsch Felix	Portfolio Coordinator	GIZ (German Agency for International Cooperation)
Felbes Hans Reudolf	Deputy Director	Swiss Cooperation
Private Sector		
Betoloum Alexis	Executive Director	Association of Microfinance Professionals
Ibrahim Adoum	Risk Manager	Agricultural Bank of Chari
Annour Djidda	Head of Studies and Planning	Housing Bank, Chad
Noubasra Natolban	Managing General	United Bank for Africa, Chad
Ouang Rebele	Managing General	SAFAR Assurances
Castro Jean-Marie	Managing General	Breweries of Chad
Allahisem Bienvenu	President's Representative	National Council of Chadian Employers
Colette Dinguimbaye	Managing General	Providence Clinique
Habib Ibn Arabi	Deputy Managing General	Ecobank Chad
Moustapha Ali Abakar	Finance Manager	Société Générale, Chad
Civil Society		
Mbairiss N. Blaise	General Secretary	Chad Teachers' Union
Brahim Ben Seid	General Secretary	Chad Free Confederation of Workers
Younouss Abdoulaye	Teacher-Researcher and SDG Focal Point	University of N'Djamena
Themoi Demsou	Teacher-Researcher	University of N'Djamena
Awat Hissein Mahamat	Teacher-Researcher	University of N'Djamena
Assadek Ibrahim	Student	University of N'Djamena
Gag Arnaud	National Coordinator	
Alhoroum Ningayo	Chief of Mission	Recovery Center for Deprived Children in Chad (CREDT)